GILL'S IRISH

C. S. PARNELL

PAUL BEW

GILL AND MACMILLAN

First published 1980 by
Gill and Macmillan Ltd
15/17 Eden Quay
Dublin 1
with associated companies in
London, New York, Delhi, Hong Kong,
Johannesburg, Lagos, Melbourne,
Singapore, Tokyo

0 7171 0963 1 (paperback)

0 7171 1079 6 (hardback)

To Greta

Origination by Healyset, Dublin
Printed in Great Britain by
Redwood Burn Ltd.
Trowbridge & Esher.

Contents

Chronology

Main Events in the Life of C. S. Parnell

1846
27 June   Birth

1869   Rusticated from Cambridge University

1875
April   Parnell returned to the House of Commons
                       as Home Rule MP for Meath

1877—78   Involved in campaign of 'obstruction' in
                       the British parliament

1877—79   Poor harvests; decreasing demand for agri-
                       cultural produce, prices falling: the estab-
                       lishment of the necessary preconditions for
                       an agrarian agitation.

1879
8 June   Parnell addresses land reform meeting at
                       Westport
21 October   Irish National Land League founded with
                       Parnell as president

1880
January—March   Parnell and Dillon on tour in America
March—April   General election: Gladstone and Liberals
                       defeat Conservatives
17 May   Parnell elected chairman of the Irish Parlia-
                       mentary Party by 23 votes to 18 out of a
                       total of 59 MPs
30 July   Parnell meets Katharine O'Shea, estranged
                       wife of a member of his own party, Captain
                       W. H. O'Shea
19 September   Advocates policy of social ostracism in
                       speech at Ennis

| 17 October | Writes to Mrs O'Shea as 'My dearest love' |
| 2 November | Parnell and leaders of Land League prosecuted (jury fails to agree, 25 January 1881) [v] |

1881

2 March	Protection of Person and Property (Ireland) Act: the British government's coercive response to the land agitation
22 August	Land Law (Ireland) Act, with provision for fair rent, fixity of tenure and free sale, and for the establishment of the Land Commission: the British government's concession to the land agitation.
15–18 September	National convention of Land League: Parnell successfully urges the convention to 'test the act'
13 October	Parnell arrested
18 October	'No rent' manifesto issued by Parnell and other imprisoned leaders
20 October	Land League suppressed

1882

February	Mrs O'Shea has her first child by Parnell
2 May	The 'Kilmainham Treaty': Parnell and other leaders released
6 May	The Phoenix Park murders
7 October	Irish National League founded

1885

| November | General election: Liberals win 335 seats, Conservatives 249, and the Parnellites 86 |
| December | The 'Hawarden Kite': Gladstone indicates that he is moving towards Home Rule |

1886

January	Irish and Liberal MPs combine to put the Conservatives out of government
February	The 'Galway Mutiny': Parnell foists Captain O'Shea on a reluctant Irish constituency against the wishes of his lieutenants
8 April	Gladstone introduces his Government of Ireland Bill (Home Rule Bill). His object is to establish an Irish legislature, although large imperial issues are to be reserved to the Westminster parliament.

June	The Home Rule Bill defeated by forty votes on the second reading
December	Parnell conveys to William O'Brien his cool attitude towards the new agrarian movement, the Plan of Campaign.

1887

March	*The Times* begins to publish its famous articles 'Parnellism and Crime'

1888

July	The government establishes a Special Commission: effectively its terms of reference place the whole Nationalist movement on trial

1889

21 February	Pigott, the forger of the *Times* letters, collapses under Charles Russell's cross-examination at the Special Commission.
8 March	Parnell shakes hands with Lord Spencer, the Lord Lieutenant at the time of the Phoenix Park murders, at the Eighty Club in London. This handshake is the public symbol of the Liberal—Nationalist alliance.
18 December	Parnell visits Gladstone at Hawarden to discuss the possible shape of a Home Rule settlement. Immediately afterwards at Liverpool Parnell speaks in the most favourable terms of the Liberal leader.
24 December	Captain O'Shea files a petition for divorce from his wife, citing Parnell as the co-respondent

1890

November	The O'Shea case comes to court
1–6 December	The Committee Room Fifteen debate: the Irish Party splits, with the majority opposed to Parnell
22 December	Parnell's candidate defeated in the North Kilkenny by-election

1891

3 April	Parnell's candidate defeated in the North Sligo by-election

Acknowledgments

In his Cambridge lectures some years ago Edward Norman first provoked my interest in Parnell. Since embarking on this biography I have incurred a number of debts. My family supported me loyally and materially. In particular, I wish to thank Roy Foster for his very kind advice. Tony Morris, Henry Patterson and Séamus Loughlin were again helpful. Colm Croker's scholarship was quite simply indispensable. I would like once again to thank the staffs of the British Museum newspaper library, Colindale, and the Linenhall Library, Belfast. My greatest debt is to Greta Jones, whose book this is.

Department of Modern History
The Queen's University of Belfast
December 1979

In years to come someone will write a book on how a great imposture can be maintained — on how to delude and dupe a nation. . . . We can speak with some personal authority. . . . We did three months in Kilmainham with Parnell. . . . He has always been the creature and puppet of the people around him.

JASPER TULLY, leading anti-Parnellite,
Roscommon Herald, 13 Dec. 1890

The strangest of all the delusions about Parnell was one amazingly rife at the time of the 'Split', that he was a greatly overrated leader, a *fainéant* who sucked the brains of his abler lieutenants. The present writer was much keelhauled at that crisis for suggesting that Parnell would be missed for many a calamitous year.

WILLIAM O'BRIEN,
The Parnell of Real Life (1926)

Foreword

There have been three great epochs of crisis in Anglo-Irish relations since the Great Famine. These were the agrarian revolution and Home Rule crises of the 1880s; the period from the Easter Rising of 1916 to the Anglo-Irish Treaty of 1921; and the Ulster 'troubles' which erupted in 1968 and are still prevalent. Yet only one of these was dominated by one Irish politician — the nationalist leader of the 1880s, C. S. Parnell, whose fall in 1891 significantly altered the content of the 'Irish question' as it existed in his time.

Parnell's career was marked by a dramatic contrast. In 1885—86 he played a decisive role in bringing about the conversion of the British premier, W. E. Gladstone, to the cause of Home Rule for Ireland. This development was almost inconceivable when Parnell entered parliament in 1875. By early 1891 Parnell's tremendous prestige had crashed following the revelations of a divorce court hearing. Yet in both moments — in defeat as in victory — Parnell displayed the same basic quality: remarkable tenacity of purpose.

This quality was displayed in his active promotion of the land and Home Rule movements. It was displayed also in the tragic conflict following the O'Shea divorce suit which ended his career. It was, indeed, precisely the same element of his character that enabled him to raise the Home Rule movement to a pitch of unprecedented success as made it possible for him in the last few months to face undaunted disasters and humiliations of the most excruciating kind. Defeat and death did not come before it was clear that

Parnell had rendered significant services to the cause
[2] of Irish nationalism.

Ever since his death Parnell has remained a remarkably potent symbol, particularly in times of
crisis and conflict in Ireland. The myth has ob-
scured the man and makes it difficult for us to see
Parnell as he really was. The difficulty has, if anything, increased with the passage of time, for the old
myth has been assailed by the creation of a new one,
so that Parnell requires a double demythologising.
For some time now he has been rescued, and rightly
so, from those who, like Pearse, sought to link him
with the separatist tradition. However, this has been
done at the price of neglecting significant aspects of
Parnell's early political strategy which alarmed not
only Unionists but also moderate Home Rulers.

The present phase of upheaval and turmoil in Irish
politics has seen the development of a new and more
critical attitude to Parnell. In particular, he has been
condemned for his alleged failure to recognise the full
significance of the Ulster Unionist opposition to
Home Rule. This view has not always been held. In
the 1920s, like today a period of political discord and
civil disturbance in Ireland, Parnell stood for a lost
stability. He represented the idea that Irish unity did
indeed once lie within the bounds of possibility and
that both unity and autonomy might have been gained
through an honourable compromise with Britain. Not
surprisingly, therefore, there was an upsurge of interest in Parnell in the 1920s, and a number of bio-
graphies appeared, including one published in 1925
by the Ulster Protestant St John Ervine. Commenting
on this popular work in 1926, Parnell's old lieutenant
William O'Brien wrote in his own *The Parnell of Real
Life:*

The demand for Mr St John Ervine's book gives us

all a startling reminder that Parnell remains an even more powerful factor of contemporary history [3] than he was when a more or less remorseful nation saw his coffin pass a generation ago. . . . He lived to the eve of a resounding Home Rule victory. . . . That victory he would have been able to turn to account as no man who has come after him can hope to do.

Was O'Brien's view merely sentimental? Are we justified in assuming that Parnell, though a Protestant himself, failed to grasp the depth of Protestant opposition to Home Rule? How great a blow was the loss of Parnell to Irish politics? How, in short, does his reputation stand today? and how ought it to stand? It is hoped in the course of this biography to answer these questions and to offer a new assessment of 'the Chief'.

1

'The Accident of Birth'

Aristocratic and autocratic as he [Parnell] was he could
not recognise anything but chance in the arrangement of
things. The accident of birth was everything.

A contemporary opinion cited by R. BARRY O'BRIEN,
The Life of Charles Stewart Parnell (1898)

1

Thomas Parnell, grandson of the mayor of Congleton
in Cheshire, established the Parnell family in Ireland,
when soon after the Restoration (1660) he bought an
estate in Queen's County. The early record of the line
in their new country did not greatly impress local
nationalist opinion. *The Nation* in 1876 said of the
eighteenth-century Parnells: 'Their love for Ireland
was negative — a passive species of affection which
seconded not the efforts of the Government of the
island in its acts of oppressive cruelty.'[1] Fortunately
for its most famous member, Charles Stewart Parnell,
the record apparently improved by the beginning of
the nineteenth century. His great-grandfather, Sir
John Parnell, opposed the Act of Union in 1800, and
this cost him his post as Chancellor of the Irish Exche-
quer. In fact Sir John's patriotism, while sound enough
if one accepts the purely eighteenth-century equation
of Irish nation and the Protestant ascendancy, did not
embrace Catholic Emancipation. This did not stop
C. S. Parnell later exploiting his record as an 'incorrup-
tible' when he entered politics. The less agreeable
aspects of Sir John's politics were simply glossed over.

It is likely, however, that a more potent influence
on Charles Stewart Parnell was the attractive liberal
patriotism of his grandfather, William Parnell, who
inherited the Avondale estate in Co. Wicklow in

1795, was MP for Wicklow from 1817 to 1820, and wrote among other works a novel, *Maurice and* [5] *Berghetta* (1819), which suggested the need for reform of Irish rural life and concessions to the Catholics.

In accordance with the now established family tradition, C. S. Parnell's father, John Henry Parnell, was a man of generous liberal political temperament. John Henry Parnell died in 1859 when his son was thirteen. Charles's American mother, who survived her husband by almost forty years, is often credited with the work of turning her son's mind against the British. Delia Tudor Stewart Parnell was the daughter of Admiral Stewart, popularly known as 'Old Ironsides', who had captured two British ships during the Anglo-American conflict of 1812. She had been a society belle in New York and Boston, and it seems likely that she was more than a little disappointed by life in rural Ireland, where she endured eleven confinements in rapid succession. Perhaps it is true that something of Parnell's disdain for precedence and defiance of authority may be traced to his maternal American republican roots. But it must not be forgotten that although Mrs Parnell kept a 'patriotic' house, her disregard for convention did not prevent her presenting her daughters at Queen Victoria's court. Moreover, if mother and daughters had Fenian leanings in the 1860s, Parnell himself was decidedly unsympathetic to the 'so-called Fenians' who called at their Dublin home.

It is hard to resist the conclusion that the contribution of Parnell's parents to his later political development was important, albeit in a negative way. Parnell's father passed on an essentially decent reformist liberalism. His mother passed on a vague (and inconsistent) American republicanism. But the really important fact about Parnell's early life is that neither of his parents shared the traditional Protestant supremacism of many sections of the Irish landlord class. This did not mean that Parnell automatically became the leader of Irish nationalism — far from it — but it did mean that this was a potential development: Parnell was able to rebel against his *class* in his political life without rebelling against his family.

2

At Avondale, a 'square, very ordinary-looking building' placed in beautiful surroundings, a mere ten minutes' walk from the famous Vale of Avoca, Charles Stewart Parnell was born on 27 June 1846. He was what is called in Ireland a bold child, his naughtiness being redeemed somewhat by a deep affection for his sisters Emily and Fanny and his brother John. 'Master Charley is born to rule,' said his nurse prophetically. However, the family was less than charmed by his domineering ways. At a mere six years of age he was sent away to a girls' school in Yeovil, Somerset. Following a severe bout of typhoid in his second term he had to be brought home. This does not seem to have sapped his strength of will. In the early 1860s Charles attended the Rev. Alexander Whishaw's private school at Chipping Norton, Oxfordshire. Whishaw's academy was a crammer for Cambridge University, and Parnell, not surprisingly, rebelled vigorously against the sterile routine. There is little doubt that his apparent arrogance made him unpopular with both boys and masters. Whatever learning be acquired, he bore it lightly.

It is not too much to say that he was quite without literary accomplishments. This weakness was disguised by the fact that his colleagues and (in later years) Mrs O'Shea composed many of his communications for him. He once showed Henry Labouchere a letter that he contemplated sending to *The Times*. The English Radical MP recorded (1891): 'This was his [7] own unaided composition, and never in my life did I see more astonishing English — confused, ungrammatical and passing comprehension.' On the other hand, J. A. Blake, a visitor to the Parnell household, detected in the pale, delicate fourteen-year-old a strong interest in science. Parnell was to retain this interest in practical scientific matters throughout his life.

After these rather desultory educational experiences Parnell went to the hearty, philistine and (at that time) academically undistinguished Magdalene College of Cambridge University from 1865 to 1869. There he does seem to have acquired a certain sense of being Irish — albeit in a very specific if perfectly legitimate sense — and most certainly *not* English. It was not at this stage a nationalistic sentiment which embraced all classes of Irishmen. 'For God's sake, John', he told his brother in 1871, 'don't tell them we are from Ireland, as they have never seen a real Irish gentleman and wouldn't know one if they did.' (J. H. Parnell, 1916, p. 90) Parnell developed a sharp dislike of what he saw as the hypocrisy of the English. He was rusticated from Cambridge University following his involvement in a drunken rowdy incident, and this may have intensified his feelings. Whatever the cause, it is certain how he felt: "He hated the English character for its innate assumption of superiority and its hypocritical pretensions to honesty and goodness.' (Kettle, 1958, p. 34)

After this negative and intellectually fruitless experience at Cambridge he returned to Ireland to take up again the pursuits of the Irish country gentleman. His prowess as a cricketer, grouse-shooter and estate-improver marked him out as an ideal candidate for the comfortable but active life of a Wicklow country squire. The Avondale estate was situated in the ancient gold-bearing region of Ireland, and although the gold [8] deposits had been practically exhausted in prehistoric times, the possibility of further discoveries remained a lifelong dream with Parnell and led to numerous prospecting operations on his part. In general, he seems to have relished the pastimes of the Irish country gentleman and to have fitted in well. Thus did affairs proceed — pleasantly enough but lethargically by any standards.

He was a well-made, handsome young man. (Most observers were impressed by the power of his eyes except Labouchere, who described them as 'fishy'.) He was capable of exercising considerable charm when he wished to do so. He may have thought that these advantages, combined with his social position, guaranteed him an interesting and successful life. If so, he was soon to receive a rude surprise.

In 1871 Parnell spent a few months in America, where he wooed a certain Miss Woods. After some early success he was rebuffed. Once again as in Cambridge, the world had shown itself to be less than overwhelmed by the young Wicklow squire. His brother, John Howard Parnell (p. 130), often a sound judge, noted: 'His jilting undoubtedly helped to drive his energies into politics, for he was deeply hurt at the idea of being considered a country gentleman without any special abilities.' Charles decided to draw on the family inheritance — which meant exploiting its social position and reputation for patriotism. The Ballot Act of 1872 decreased the costs of political campaigning, and the possibility that he might enter politics began to crop up for discussion in the family circle. Suddenly in 1874 a bored and restless Parnell took the decision and sought out the leaders of the Home Rule movement. The moment had arrived for Parnell's prolonged, if pleasant, adolescence to come to an end.

His early ventures were hardly a success. He had to put up his brother John for Wicklow, as his own position as High Sheriff of the county ruled out his candidature there. John was, however, defeated. Charles himself stood in Dublin in 1874 and was also defeated. Finally, in 1875 he won a seat for Meath. In all these campaigns great emphasis was laid on the family's patriotic record.

3

The decision to enter politics had its bad side. Parnell's family had a reputation for mental disorder as well as patriotism. He was more than aware of this. 'Madness', he often said, was not a word the Parnells used lightly. The effort of self-control required was enormous. He was at first a wretched public speaker — the possessor, incidentally, of a strong English accent. After his first unsuccessful campaign for Dublin Parnell collapsed with a nervous illness for six weeks. His closest colleagues noted a tendency to clench his fists so hard while speaking as to leave the marks of his nails. Moreover, all this was compounded by the fact that Parnell was intensely superstitious. One part of his superstition was a loathing for the colour green. This was obviously not an advantage for an Irish leader who frequently had to speak from public platforms draped with green flags and decorations. (The House of Commons, it should not be forgotten, was upholstered in the same offensive hue.) In short, the young Parnell appeared to be a bundle of barely controlled contradictions. He was febrile, tense, and yet withal assertive.

For we should not forget his already evident strength of will: to emphasise only the neurotic aspects of Parnell's personality is a great mistake. He seems to have regarded his public nervousness as merely something that had to be overcome. There is [10] no sign that he was given to agonising bouts of self-appraisal. Indeed, his colleagues marvelled at his apparent lack of self-consciousness. T. P. O'Connor (1887, p. 150) described him as a neither 'expansive nor introspective. It is one of the strongest and most curious peculiarities of Mr Parnell not merely that he rarely, if ever, speaks of himself but that he rarely, if ever, gives any indication of having studied himself. . . . It is a joke among his intimates that to Mr Parnell the being Parnell does not exist.' Parnell, it should be stressed, was an upper-class country gentleman, with much of the assurance — and occasional toughness — of his class. Labouchere's obituary (1891) is worth recalling:

> A selfish man Parnell certainly was, but he was good-naturedly selfish. If anyone stood in his way, he would sacrifice him without a moment's hesitation, nor would he go greatly out of his way to serve a friend. When, however, his own interest was not concerned, he would not put himself out to do either friend or foe an injury. Politeness has been defined as good nature in little things, and this sort of good nature he had.

A combination of boredom and disappointment seems to have pushed Parnell into politics. Once involved, he brought to bear considerable qualities of determination, though not, it is said, imagination. 'The strength of Parnell was character rather than intellect,' wrote T. P. O'Connor (1891, p. 221) in a typical phrase. John Morley (quoted in Robbins, 1926, p. 18) in a similar fashion called him a 'man of temperament, of will, of authority, of power, not of ideas or ideals, or knowledge or political maxims, or even of practical reason in its higher senses'. It is true that Parnell was no intellectual in the way that T. P.

or Morley were. He avoided the 'arts' and much pre-
ferred dogs, horses and the sports and pastimes of [11]
the countryside as a means of relaxation. His pleas-
ures were as uncomplicated as those of any country
squire. It is hard to imagine a man more different
from those who were to be his principal lieutenants:
Justin McCarthy, Tim Healy, T. P. O'Connor, Thomas
Sexton, John Dillon and William O'Brien. While they
were sociable, articulate speakers and inveterate
scribblers, Parnell was the reverse. And yet for all
that Parnell was no intellectual in this conventional
sense, he was not, as is so often suggested, a mere
technician of power. He made a contribution to Irish
political debate which was as important as it was
unique.

To understand this we have to understand that
Parnell had a particular view of the Anglo-Irish
dilemma and that this view conditioned his politics
in the strongest possible way. Parnell, always said to
be the most 'pragmatic' of politicians, is not explicable
without reference to this ideological dimension. In
short, he did not do all his thinking on his feet.

The idea that Parnell lacked a notion of the Anglo-
Irish past — which is not, of course, the same thing as
precise historical knowledge — has been an essential
part of the picture constructed by those who see him
as a 'hollow man' or an empty vessel. Deprived of his
assumptions about this aspect of Irish history — and
most importantly, of his sense of his own place and
role in its unfolding — Parnell is easily distorted. His
success becomes largely a matter of good fortune. It
is child's play then to interpret his career as the
sacked Cambridge undergraduate indulging his bile
against the English who have failed to treat him with
due regard.

There were indeed many at the time who saw
Parnell as purely opportunistically activated by a

hatred for England rather than a love for Ireland. [12] There is even an element of truth in this picture. After his adoption of a firm nationalist political stance Parnell began to emphasise certain aspects of his experience that were to hand — 'patriotic' ancestors, Wicklow stories of English atrocities in 1798, the meaning of the Fenian rising of 1867 — in a novel way. But for a long time these influences had lain dormant in his psyche. After his decision to enter politics he made use of them to create an almost poetically satisfying effect. We need not accept all the elements of the Parnell myth. But to treat him simply as a man who used politics as a means of expression for his personal resentments is grossly unfair. This can be seen clearly when his attitude to the Anglo-Irish tradition is explored.

Parnell made not the slightest effort to hide his lack of enthusiasm for Gaelic culture (Healy, II, p. 401). He appears to have had a somewhat greater interest in the more general aspects of Irish history. At any rate he turned up to a lecture on the subject in Dublin in July 1878 and felt it right to condemn the neglect of Irish history in Irish schools in January 1885. Michael Davitt (1904, p. 114) generously claimed that Parnell had a fair historical knowledge. But Mrs O'Shea and others who knew him well were less sure. An American reporter who visited him in the last year of his life recorded of his library: 'Very few political works are to be seen. Metallurgy, geology and astronomy are his chief delights.'[2] This has the ring of truth. Parnell's 'sense of history' was not derived from book-learning. Nevertheless, almost as a family inheritance, he had an acute insight into the schizophrenia of the Anglo-Irish condition.

The Anglo-Irish, conscious that they were a privileged minority, separated by race and religion from those whose land their ancestors had seized, still

looked to England as their ultimate protector and
regarded themselves as members of an empire which
they were proud to serve. At the same time they felt
themselves to be Irish. This divided loyalty led them
eventually into the characteristic predicament of a
colonial governing class, torn between their country
of origin and their country of settlement (Lyons,
1979, pp. 18—19). This was the essence of the Anglo-
Irish heritage, of which Parnell was so intensely aware.
It determined his view of the past; more importantly,
it shaped his hopes for the future.

4

Parnell was remarkably consistent in his appraisal of
the Irish question. Considering it, naturally enough,
from a specifically Anglo-Irish standpoint, not only
was he conscious of the part played by his own class
in the evolution of the problem, but he was also convinced that this class had an important role to play in
its solution. The Act of Union had created an incen-
tive for landlords to look to England to maintain
their dominant and yet precarious position in Irish
society. Parnell did not hold, as his Catholic lieutenants tended to, that the landlord class was in any
literal sense a garrison class; it had ceased to have any
such claims before 1850. But he did hold that the
landlords looked to England as the guarantor of their
exalted status and that it was in consequence of this
that they opposed nationalist politics. The way forward was to fight for progressive reforms, particularly
land reforms, which removed the privileges of the
Irish landlords and *removed simultaneously the
barrier to their association in the Home Rule movement.* The disestablishment of the Church of Ireland,
which seemed to prompt some degree of Protestant
involvement in the Home Rule agitation in the early
1870s, seemed to be a proof of Parnell's general case.

In a hastily researched address to the Young Ireland Society in Cork in 1885 he considered what Ireland had suffered in the nineteenth century as a result of the loss of her native parliament. He argued that had Grattan's Parliament been retained, a number of benefits would have followed:

> It would also have been better for both people and the owners of land — the landowners in Ireland. They would have been taught to conciliate the people towards them; they would have learned to govern the people justly and uprightly, and to give them by degrees those larger privileges, the extension of the franchise to the masses of the people, the right for all sections to vote and take their places as members for constituencies which it has taken eighty-four years of struggling to obtain (hear, hear). I cannot doubt that much mischief would have been spared, and that instead of occupying the humiliating position which the landlord class now do, they would have a better and happier one.[3]

Parnell's view of the history of the relations between the owners and occupiers of land during the nineteenth century clearly implied that the landlords were an exposed body. He felt that they ought to reach a rapprochement with the Irish democracy before it was too late and that such a rapprochement should of necessity include a general measure of land reform. His conspectus therefore inclined him towards a radical position on the land question.

And here a matter of personal history has to be entered into the record. As early as 1871 Parnell was not really the well-to-do country gentleman of appearances. His affairs were in fact running towards an increasing debt. His recently discovered letters for the period 1875—78 reveal him as an exceptionally benevolent landlord, but they also further display the chaotic state of his personal finances (Raymond, [15] 1980). Parnell's readiness to accept changes in the old land system is surely linked to the fact that it had never proved profitable in his own case. Of course, many Irish landlords similarly burdened by mortgages fought passionately to maintain the old society, but why they did so — as the memoirs of Parnell's sister Anna mordantly testify — remained something of a mystery to the Parnell family. Parnell was convinced that it was better for everyone, landlords and tenants alike, if the land system was reformed.

The irony of a Protestant landlord leading a militantly anti-landlord movement composed of the Catholic democracy was not lost on contemporaries. Parnell's advocacy of land reform and Home Rule led many landed families to see him as a traitor. For his part Parnell felt that Ireland should be governed by the men of substance *who lived in it.* In this sense he was indeed perhaps the last representative of those Protestant gentlemen who had appealed for an autonomous Ireland in the age of Grattan. 'On one occasion when I spent a night at his house in Avondale', recalled T. P. O'Connor (1929, I, p. 99), 'I could not help remarking on the tattered banners that hung from the ceiling of the lofty hall, all belonging to the period and struggles that immediately preceded the destruction of the Irish Parliament in 1800.'

Parnell was undoubtedly a liberalised scion of this tradition. But how was he to reconcile the claims of a nationalism backed by the Catholic democracy with his essential social conservatism? This was to be the basic underlying question of Parnell's career.

2

'On the Verge of Treason-Felony'

He saw as if by instinct that Fenianism was the key of
Irish nationality. . . . We shall therefore see him as the
years roll by standing on the verge of treason-felony.
                    R. BARRY O'BRIEN (1898) on Parnell in 1875

1

The Irish political scene in the mid-1870s was dominated by Isaac Butt's Home Rule League which had
been formed in 1873. Butt and the majority of his
followers devoted their energies to an unfailingly
polite and almost totally ineffective parliamentary
campaign to advance the Irish case for a moderate
degree of self-government. Whatever his reservations
about this line of action, Parnell, on deciding to enter
politics in the nationalist interest, had little choice
but to attempt to become a Home Rule MP.

Parnell's intermediary in obtaining the blessings of
the committee which selected him as candidate for
Meath was Patrick Egan, a figure who later acquired
an extremist and even sinister reputation. Egan had
been a Fenian since the 1860s and was to be linked
with political violence in the 1880s. However, it should
be remembered that in the 1870s Egan, like many
other Fenians, was willing to give the Home Rule
movement a serious and honest try. His convictions
on this point are clear. It would be difficult to over-
stress the umbrella nature of the movement Isaac
Butt led. Furthermore, Patrick Egan performed services not only for Parnell but also for many other
Home Rule figures, including Colonel King-Harman,
later a Conservative Under-Secretary for Ireland, for
whom he wrote election addresses.[1] Not too much
should therefore be made of the 'extreme' nature of
Parnell's early sponsorship.

In this context it should also be added that Parnell heavily relied on that respectable anti-Fenian body, the Catholic clergy of Meath, in his campaign. The local newspaper noted: 'Mr Parnell had all the Roman Catholic clergy at his back and they publicly were the chief agents in his election.'[2] It was said at the time, though denied, that the clergy had agreed to support one of Parnell's opponents, J. T. Hinds, and then reneged on him.

However, Parnell's references to nationalism were more decisive than in his earlier Dublin campaign. He spoke airily of England's weakness some day becoming Ireland's opportunity. This may well have been partly due to the fact that his two unsuccessful opponents, J. T. Hinds and J. L. Napper, subscribed to some form of national autonomy for Ireland. As the local anti-Home Rule paper, the *Meath Herald,* commented sadly, 'A Conservative has no chance whatever of polling a majority in Meath, seeing that the county is every day becoming more and more intensely national. We believe the most outspoken candidate of the Mitchellite type will be elected.'[3] This was a reference to the former Young Irelander, John Mitchel, who had been elected for Tipperary on the eve of his death earlier in the year. Sensibly enough in view of this assessment, Parnell had publicly sent a cheque of £25 towards Mitchel's election expenses.

Parnell's election for Meath was not perceived at the time as a significant landmark. His opponents dismissed him as either a naïve young man of basically loyalist principles or as an unprincipled opportunist. In this spirit one Conservative paper commented:

Mr Parnell is one of those gentlemen, not few in number, who of later years have had their eyes suddenly opened to the paramount and pressing necessity for Home Rule and whose convictions in this direction by a curious coincidence have been awakened simultaneously with a vacancy in the parliamentary representation of some place.[4]

Nationalist sources tended rather to emphasise the canvassing energy shown by Parnell and his agent: 'Had the other candidates followed the same course their figures might be more, but Mr Parnell worked energetically all through.'[5] But they were rather vague about the precise nature of this views. At this point the question of Parnell's future political development was an absolutely open one. This situation was not, however, to last very long.

In August 1875 a significant incident revealed much about the balance of forces in Irish politics. The Lord Mayor of Dublin, Peter Paul McSwiney, attempted to exploit the celebrations of the O'Connell centenary to the exclusive advantage of those who favoured a revival of the alliance of Liberals and Catholic Church in Ireland. This new venture — 'Faith and Fatherland', as McSwiney called it — was crushed by huge crowds mobilised by the Home Rulers and Fenians. The newly elected MP for Meath had had nothing to do with all this; he did not even attend the O'Connell centenary in any capacity. However, he quickly got involved with the Lord Mayor in a row over the distribution of the centenary committee's funds. It was rather an undignified squabble and of itself can hardly have done Parnell much good: as one irritated nationalist newspaper editor commented, 'There is scarcely one man in Ireland . . . who is not sick of these wretched disputes.'[6] But the affair did make even more clear the militant nationalist drift of his views. It also showed a certain determination to catch the public eye.

His speeches were at first noted more for passion

than for coherence; his actual words often went unrecorded. A typical report of a speech at Liverpool in early 1876 runs: 'Mr Parnell was warmly applauded during a brief but animated address.'[7] A few days after this Liverpool speech Parnell attended a meeting to unveil a monument to Grattan in Dublin. Despite the Parnell family's obvious historical connections with Grattan, the new MP was not invited to speak.[8]

2

Parnell's early impact on the House of Commons was slight. Barry O'Brien (1898, I, p. 85) recorded: 'Parnell remained chiefly a calm spectator of the proceedings of the House of Commons watching, learning, biding his time.' In 1876 he did, however, suddenly come before the public eye. In a famous interruption of the Chief Secretary, he claimed that the Fenians who had accidentally killed a policeman at Manchester in 1867 while attempting to rescue two of their comrades had committed no murder. Despite the ensuing English uproar, Parnell pressed on with his chosen course of action. In particular, he made it his business to cultivate Fenian sentiment, not only in Ireland but also, and even more assiduously, in England and Scotland. The Home Rule Confederation of Great Britain was largely composed of *sotto voce* republicans, and Parnell did his best to become their favourite.

It was in association with these elements that Parnell in the autumn of 1876 launched himself on a trip to the United States. The purpose was to convey a congratulatory address to the President on the centenary of the American Declaration of Independence. The address on behalf of the 'Irish people' — in reality Irish republicans — was refused, but Parnell did gain useful public attention.

On his return, he spoke once more at Liverpool. He
was no more coherent than he had been at the beginning of 1876. 'He was a bad speaker then — had a bad
halting delivery. In fact, it was painful to listen.'
Nevertheless, he was now regarded with some serious-
ness. 'He shook nervously until the word he wanted
came. . . . Parnell's word was always the right word
and expressed exactly the idea in his head.' (R. B.
O'Brien, I, p. 102) More precisely, he expressed
exactly the idea in the collective head of his audience.

From this point on, we can watch Parnell steadily
build up his rapport with militant Irish nationalist
sentiment in England and Scotland. He insisted that
nothing was to be gained by conciliating England:

> Why was some measure of protection given to
> the Irish tenant? Why was the English Church
> [sic] disendowed and disestablished?
>
> A VOICE: The Fenians did that; it was not the Home
> Rulers.
>
> MR PARNELL: No, the gentleman is right. It was
> not the Home Rulers. He was afraid that the
> Irish members could go on for a long time at
> their present gait before they ever do anything
> for Ireland. These things were obtained because
> there was an explosion at Clerkenwell, and an
> attack upon the police van at Manchester.[9]

At a later Scottish meeting at Dumbarton Parnell's
attitude was similar. A militant republican revolutionary named Daly led a group who attempted to break
up the gathering of 'constitutionalists'. There was very
considerable uproar; but, as William O'Malley (1891)
later recalled, 'Parnell calmly looked on, and turning
to an Irish *priest* beside him and myself remarked,
"Perhaps Daly is right," meaning that possibly physical force would be the best means to secure Irish freedom.'

In the parliamentary session of 1877 Parnell threw himself into the project known as 'obstruction'. In itself there was nothing particularly original about the idea of delaying parliamentary business by prolonged and irrelevant speech-making during debates. Even Isaac Butt, the moderate Home Rule leader, had condoned the practice in 1875 on the occasion of an Irish coercion bill. However, despite Butt's reproofs, Parnell and his allies, the ungracious Belfast pork merchant Joseph Gillis Biggar and the pockmarked 'workhouse boy' John O'Connor Power (both of whom were under sentence of expulsion from the Irish Republican Brotherhood at this time for their participation in constitutional politics), did not restrict themselves to blocking Irish legislation but widened the scope of the tactic to cover imperial concerns. This defiant activity reached its high point in July 1877 with a twenty-six hours' sitting on the South Africa Bill.

Thanks to such work, it was clear by early or mid-1877 Parnell was the effective leader of the Irish in England and Scotland. His deposition of Butt as President of the Home Rule Confederation of Great Britain in the autumn merely ratified this situation. It is often suggested that Parnell's reaction to Butt's fall was somewhat cold-hearted. But as the political commentator Count Roman Zubof (1891) wrote, 'I have been told by Mr John Ferguson of Glasgow, an intimate friend of Mr Parnell's . . . that when the old organiser of Home Rule, broken-hearted, walked out of the room . . . there was not a man there more touched than Mr Parnell.' Parnell made it a point never to allow personal emotion for others to interfere in his politics. As Kettle (1958, p. 35) explained, 'I might mention . . . that we both agreed from the beginning of our acquaintance that all men and all things were to be used in the most impersonal manner

to work out the desired end.' From the moment of
[22] Parnell's arrival as a major force in political life it was
clear that Butt's role in Irish politics was over and
that the Home Rule movement had lost its way. If
the movement was to cease being an ineffectual force,
the fall of Butt was a political necessity.

It should also be noted that in the summer of 1877
Parnell's work in England and Scotland began to pay
off at home. In August 1877 we find a really vigorous demonstration for Parnell *in Ireland*. At a meeting in Dublin Parnell 'was received with extraordinary enthusiasm. The whole audience rose to their
feet, with waving of hats and handkerchiefs, and the
cheering was repeated again and again for nearly ten
minutes.'[10] Parnell had definitely arrived. It was the
beginning of a rapport with Dublin nationalists which
was broken only by his death.

3

It is interesting to gauge the reaction within rural
Ireland to the policy of obstruction in parliament.
The first public body to support this policy was the
Ballinasloe Tenants' Defence Association — very much
an association of small farmers with a strong tendency
to engage in anti-grazier, anti-rancher rhetoric.[11] On
the other hand, bodies like the Limerick Farmers'
Club, whose members were proud to call themselves
'big graziers', tended to be lukewarm in their attitude
to militant nationalist politics and deeply suspicious
of the organised activities of small farmers. Accord-
ingly their initial sympathies lay with Butt,[12] who, it
was assumed, would eventually tackle the question of
land reform at some future date; however, partly as a
result of the deteriorating agricultural conditions
after 1878, even this affluent class of tenants belatedly
came to support the policy of obstruction.

Parnell, naturally enough, was drawn towards those who had first given him support in Ireland. He began to take a lively interest in the problems of the smaller tenantry. At the end of 1877 Parnell made a trip to Mayo in the company of his fellow-obstructionist O'Connor Power. This visit has received scant attention from historians, but it was nevertheless of some significance. For although the meeting he addressed was not particularly well attended, the particular attitudes and problems of Mayo impressed themselves firmly on his mind. He gained a general assurance of support but also a sense of particular regional grievances. James Daly, the locality's leading journalist, recorded: 'Mr Parnell left Mayo deeply impressed that [his] Parliamentary policy was endorsed by the people of Mayo and also that the land bill was required to give the tenantry some stability in the soil *as well as to encourage the reclamation of the waste lands of Ireland* [my italics].'[13] Parnell later recalled: 'From the first I ever came to the West of Ireland I have been taught valuable and immortal lessons.'[14]

This emphasis on reclamation is important because it indicates Parnell's early awareness of a problem that was to play a very significant role in his politics in later years. The West required not only 'fixity of tenure' — the normal measure of land reform required for the rest of Ireland — it required also reclamation of waste lands. This indicates the nature of the crucial problem for many tenants in the West: what they needed was not a reduction of rent on their pitifully small and barren holdings but *more land*. (Even a large rent reduction would only be a sop.) Only such a measure would really solve the social question in the West. The only means of indicating this in 1877 was to advocate reclamation of waste lands. In the more hopeful atmosphere generated by the Land

League in 1880 these tenants were prepared to de-
[24] mand explicitly the redistribution of the large grazing
holdings in the area.

Parnell's public flirtation with Fenianism was linked
to a series of private meetings with Irish republican
leaders. As early as August 1877 he had managed to
make a very favourable impression on a prominent
figure, James J. O'Kelly, who declared to John Devoy:
'He has many of the qualities of leadership — and time
will give him more. He is cool — extremely so and
resolute.' (O'Brien and Ryan, 1948—53, I, pp. 267—8)
By the beginning of 1878 he had managed to convince Dr William Carroll, another leader, of his adher-
ence to the principle of absolute independence whilst
avoiding any commitment to the Fenian movement as
such. In fact the increasing hopelessness of the traditional militarist dream of an armed uprising to drive
out the English predisposed the more realistic separ-
atists to give Parnell a good hearing. Not that he was
saying much. At a second meeting in March 1878 he
remained largely silent. He could afford to. The separ-
atists were gradually dropping the idea of making
Parnell one of their number. Instead they were beginning to think in terms of how they could most profit-
ably assist Parnell.

John Devoy, the most capable and serious of the
Irish-American militants, made this clear in a telegram
on 25 October 1878 when he offered Parnell the
'New Departure' package. Parnell had just been re-
elected President of the Home Rule Confederation of
Great Britain with Fenian support and Devoy felt —
wrongly, as it turned out — that this was a moment of
crucial importance. However, the important thing to
note is that he offered Parnell the support of American
militants on certain conditions:

(1) Abandonment of the federal demand and substitu-
tion of a general demand in favour of self-government.

(2) Vigorous agitation of the land question on the basis of a peasant proprietary, while accepting concessions tending to abolish arbitrary eviction.

(3) Exclusion of all sectarian issues from the platform.

(4) Party members to vote together on all imperial and home questions, adopt an aggressive policy and energetically resist coercive legislation.

(5) Advocacy of all struggling nationalities in the British Empire or elsewhere.

Parnell made no public response to this package offer. A few days later he decided to accept an invitation from the Ballinasloe Tenants' Defence Association to speak in the West of Ireland. Shrouded as he was in an aura of republican conspiracy, it is hardly surprising to find that Parnell was not yet a completely respectable figure in Irish politics. Outside Meath the clergy regarded him warily. As James Kilmartin, the president of the Ballinasloe Tenants' Defence Association later recalled, 'The priests would not then identify with Parnell. None of them would take the chair, and only two took places on the platform.'[15]

At the meeting held at Ballinasloe on 3 November Parnell was forthright enough in his expression of views on the land question:

There were five and a half millions of people in this country, enough people to win their own freedom, and if they were determined, they would win it; they would win the land and the right of living on the soil under the landlords by paying rent, or by purchasing from the landlords and becoming possessors of their own farms *(applause)*. He himself was in favour of the latter system, which prevailed in France and Prussia, and would prevail in Ireland (hear, hear).[16]

However, perhaps in response to the chill of clerical
[26] disapproval, he retreated later in the month from his
emphasis on the principle of peasant proprietorship
and made it clear that the 'three Fs' (fair rent, fixity
of tenure, free sale) was still the object of practical
reformers.

4

But what was Parnell's precise contribution to the
debate on the land question? In particular, what was
the relationship he perceived between the land question and the national question in Ireland? This is a
matter of fundamental importance which must be
understood if Parnell's true role in Irish politics is to
be grasped. The nature of this relationship was the
subject of intense debate in the late 1870s. It is
necessary to outline this debate before it is possible
to understand the novelty of Parnell's contribution.

The basic problem lay in the fact that the British
parliament was perceived to be unalterably opposed
to Irish agrarian demands. At the end of May 1875
The Irishman reported Isaac Butt's view of the matter:
'I would be lending myself to the wildest and most
mischievous of delusions if I led you to believe that
there is any chance of the present House of Commons
passing a measure even approaching to that which
would meet the wants and wishes of the Irish occupiers.' John Devoy, for his part, put it more bluntly
five years later when he insisted that the 'demands of
the Land League will not be granted by a Parliament
of British landlords. Of course they won't.'[17]

In early 1878 William Bolster, a key figure of the
Limerick Farmers' Club, had argued that the obsession with Home Rule was leading to a neglect of the
tenant farmers' interests. He stated clearly: 'The land
question should be settled first before dealing with

the vital one of Home Rule.' John Dillon, who was just beginning his long career as a prominent nation- alist politician, was quick to criticise Bolster:

> The more discussion there is, the more plain will it appear that there can be no rivalry between Home Rule and tenant-right. The only chance of winning tenant-right is by vigorously pressing our demand for Home Rule, when a land bill may be as a sop thrown to Cerberus. And, on the other hand, a vigorous tenant-right agitation would strengthen the Home Rulers immediately.[18]

However, Dillon failed to explain the mechanism by which a vigorous tenant-right agitation would actually have strengthened the Home Rulers. This was a problem which bothered also that group of 'neo-Fenians' — of whom Michael Davitt, Patrick Egan and Thomas Brennan were the most forceful leaders — who had adopted a sympathetic attitude towards open political agitation in the 1870s. Eventually they were to solve it by declaring that as no British government would grant peasant proprietorship in Ireland, the struggle for that end would lead to the breaking of the British link. In other words, they accepted Isaac Butt's basic premise but reached a very different conclusion. For where Butt saw only grounds for a rather despairing brand of constitutional politics, the neo-Fenians deduced that there was a basis for revolutionary activity.

But Parnell was to solve the problem his own way — without being forced to adopt either the pessimism of Butt or the revolutionary principles of the neo-Fenians. He gives us the first brief hint of it in a speech delivered in Kerry on 15 November 1878:

> He had heard some people say, 'Oh I am not a Home Ruler — I am a tenant righter.' He had to say to such a man, 'I don't care what you are.' ...

There was no antagonism between them and there could be none *(cheers)*. Settle the land question on a firm basis, give the tenant farmers the right to live on their farms, level the barriers that divided class from class, and there would be no interest sufficiently strong to retain English misgovernment, and they would then have Home Rule *(cheers)*.[19]

This is the clue to the celebrated question of whether Parnell reached, as John Devoy later claimed, a 'definite agreement' with him on political principles on 1 June 1879.

Parnell did have a series of meetings with Devoy in March, April and June 1879. Devoy later claimed that a definite agreement on strategy was reached on 1 June. However, such an agreement can only have been highly notional. Parnell's priorities — those of the Anglo-Irish squire hoping to reconcile his 'own people' to nationalism — and Devoy's — those of the cottier's son who had shown a scathing disregard for the claims of the Anglo-Irish — were poles apart. Michael Davitt, who was also present, described Parnell's attitude as one of friendly neutrality towards the revolutionary movement, and this rings more true.

Parnell's argument contained three basic elements. Firstly, he clearly believed, unlike both Butt and the neo-Fenians, that it was possible to settle the land question within the framework of the United Kingdom, always providing enough pressure was applied. Secondly, this would eliminate the conflict over rent between Irish landlord and peasant. Thirdly, this would in turn create the conditions in which the Irish landlords could take their proper place as leaders of the Home Rule movement. At the very least, they would cease to use their influence against Home Rule. The nationalist movement would thus gain a new credibility and achieve victory.

Parnell was almost alone in his views. Only one man had in the public controversy of January 1878 openly developed a similar theme. Andrew Kettle of Artane, Co. Dublin, the secretary of the Central Tenants' Defence Association, had argued that a good land reform would have 'the effect of turning the occupiers from slaves into men and the owners from irresponsible autocrats into Irish gentlemen'.[20] However, apart from Kettle — with whom Parnell was often to discuss the problem in precisely these terms — the Wicklow squire's view of the problem was entirely original and idiosyncratic. By the end of 1878, therefore, Parnell had already outlined the doctrine which was to play such an important role in the land war.

But this doctrine has an important secondary implication. It cannot be denied that Parnell genuinely held it. It was not, for example, a deceit to persuade the British government that he was a moderate at heart. Parnell's numerous clear statements of this position, both in public and in private and over such a long time-span, from 1878 to the end of his career, rules out this interpretation. And in spite of its apparent eccentricity, the doctrine did have some political utility. Like his 'Grattanism', it served to mark him out from the other potential leaders of the new realignment of forces in Irish politics. It indicated a potential willingness on Parnell's part to invest the land question with a nationalist political significance. It did not matter at the time that this was totally different from the significance given it by the neo-Fenians: what really mattered was that he was available to provide leadership for the new movement. In 1878–79 the other potential New Departure leaders, F. H. O'Donnell and P. J. Smyth, refused to take this step. They regarded the land question as unrelated to the task of building up national sentiment. For Par-

nell, on the other hand, it was vital. Thus he agreed
[30] with the neo-Fenians that the land question was the
key to the national question, while at the same time
he was able to remain an honest constitutionalist. He
always insisted that the British parliament could
settle the Irish land question, but that the outcome —
the accession of the landlords to the Home Rule side
— would make the cause of Ireland irresistible. It was
therefore in a perfectly genuine sense that Parnell
could claim to be a militant nationalist but also a conservative and a constitutionalist. It was not so much
that he gave different impressions to different groups
— though, of course, he did that — but that he genuinely was all these things.

3

'A Spontaneous Uprising':
The Land League

The Land League was . . . a spontaneous uprising. . . . It
was not due, and its success was not due, to guidance or
leadership.
    PARNELL, speech at Irishtown anniversary meeting,
        1891 (*Weekly Freeman*, 25 Apr. 1891)

1

When Isaac Butt, in his early role as university professor, was examining in political economy at Trinity
College, Dublin, he regularly asked his students the
question: what limits rent?[1] In the period 1879—82
the mass of the Irish peasantry were to give a peremp-
tory but definitive answer to this question: the Land
League.

Exceptionally wet weather, crop failures and falling prices in the winter of 1878—79 threatened the rural population in the West of Ireland with the worst economic disaster since the Great Famine. But this time the general socio-political context was totally changed. There was no likelihood that the mass of the peasantry would again passively accept their fate. They wanted a rent rebate, and the more militant wanted to inflict a harder blow against landlordism. A. M. Sullivan, MP, explained:

> The agitation is much more than for remission of rent with certain of the men who are moving in the matter all over the island. With the older peasants, the unlettered drudges, the cry is merely for a momentary abatement of rent; but, my dear sir, the schoolmaster has been abroad; the National Schools and the penny newspapers have made their mark on a rural generation that has grown to manhood since '47.[2]

This new generation, Sullivan claimed, regarded the Great Famine with 'a deep, savage, mad feeling'. They were determined to see that there should not be even a localised repetition. They were determined also to settle the agricultural crisis at the expense of the landlords.

But what else were these new ideologues saying? The emphasis on self-reliance, on making the landlord bear the burden of the economic situation, is clear enough. But it has to be said that there was also available an almost utopian political and social rhetoric. The National Teacher M. M. O'Sullivan was telling the peasants of the West that they could *not* expect a satisfactory measure of land reform from their hereditary enemies in the British parliament. He did not hesitate to imply that the current struggle for land reform was also the struggle for nationalist

revolution. The penny-newspaper editor James Daly
[32] had revealed himself as the possessor of remarkable
assumptions about Irish rural life. For Daly the im-
pending economic crisis was likely to herald a collapse
of cattle farming among *all* sections of the farming
population and a massive return to tillage. This was
putting the clock back with a vengeance. He even
held the millenarian view that vast numbers of Irish-
Americans would return to enjoy the benefits of this
new economy.[3]

Not surprisingly, in the face of these currents,
Parnell's early involvement in the land agitation was
marked by an obvious hesitancy. Even after the
success of a meeting held at Irishtown, Co. Mayo,
on 20 April 1879 had indicated the obvious potential,
he still held back. It required a special effort of persuasion from Michael Davitt, at that time a separatist
activist beginning his involvement in land reform which
was to become the great theme of his life, to persuade
him to attend the second key meeting at Westport,
Co. Mayo, on 8 June 1879. Even then he was not fully
committed. In fact it was not until early November,
some days *after* the Irish National Land League
was set up in Dublin on 21 October 1879, that
Parnell as the new organisation's president committed
himself fully. He did this by signing a militant Land
League address which left no doubt that he stood with
the new movement.

Many reasons have been advanced for Parnell's
caution and indecision in the summer and autumn of
1879. Fear of a storm of clerical disapproval certainly
played some part. Parnell also took good care to find
out the views of 'respectable' strong farmers in other
parts of the country before committing himself to
an agitation which was largely at that time based on
smallholders. It was surely a basic precaution for
Parnell to determine the depth of discontent among

the stronger men. Such solicitude paid off. Parnell's concern ensured that the always potential alliance between moderate Home Rulers and the stronger farmers of the regional Farmers' Clubs failed to materialise.

But the most profound cause of Parnell's hesitation lay in a basic political difference with some key Land League leaders. Parnell did not see the land question as eventually leading to a peasant nationalist insurrection. His long-term hope is clear: a socially stable partnership between 'reformed' landlords and a 'satiated' class of peasants. This pan-class solidarity would increase the potential of nationalism. As he put it at Liverpool at the end of November 1879, 'Deprive this class [the landlords] of their privileges, show them that they must cast themselves in with the rest of their countrymen ... [and] the last knell of English power ... in Ireland has been sounded.'

It will be said that this assessment of Parnell's was naïve, and in a certain sense it was. Many members of the Irish landlord class bitterly spurned his blandishments. Yet eleven years later, near the end of his career, he still clung tenaciously to his beliefs:

We do not want to exterminate the residential Irish landlords (hear, hear), we have never felt any ill-will towards individual landlords (hear, hear). We have successfully abolished the system; we have put an end to the power of those owners — many of them victims of circumstances — to oppress and rack-rent their tenantry (hear, hear). With a suitable solution of the land question we should gladly welcome the continued presence of those gentlemen in Ireland (hear, hear). We should gladly see them taking their part for which they are fitted in the future social regeneration of this country (hear, hear), in the future direction of its affairs and in the future national life of Ireland (hear, hear).[4]

On this theoretical basis, then, Parnell committed himself to the Land League. One thing the League needed as quickly as possible was money. There was only one way of obtaining it — and that was to send its new leader to America. Before Parnell left for America in December 1879 there were fears that his aristocratic ancestry and relatively moderate policies made him an unsuitable figure to appeal to Irish-Americans. In actual fact Parnell turned out to be ideal for the purpose. Wealthy and prominent Irish-Americans who had spurned the Fenian Brotherhood were attracted by Parnell's very respectability. In New York city and Boston, where a well-to-do Irish stratum was firmly established, Parnell was gradually able to win most of this group to financial support of the Land League. This required an early moderation of tone. In New York in particular he was forced to lay emphasis on the need to collect money for relief rather than for political purposes. But this soft-pedalling approach was not necessary in other parts of the country. 'Yielding to the tone of the New York *Herald* and of Fifth Avenue opinion,' wrote the *Irish Times* special reporter covering the tour, 'Mr Parnell had begun to relegate the reform part of his programme from the first to the second place of importance in his speeches. Beyond New York there is a different state of things. It is evident that American views are really centred upon the land reform as the object of chief importance.'[5] The more typical Irish-Americans — in Philadelphia and Chicago, where the middle class was weaker, or in the militant mining regions of Pennsylvania and the western states, or in the smaller industrial centres — were passionately pro-Land League. They needed little persuasion to put their dollars at the new movement's disposal. Parnell was deeply impressed by this commitment and was later to compare it unfavourably with that of the Irish farmers themselves. He was to refer pointedly to his experience in America, where 'the hard-working Irish and American people, many of whom work ten times as hard as many Irish farmers,' showed a much greater commitment to the cause. Significantly also, as the tour progressed Parnell's views became more and more revolutionary. He was, for example, reported — perhaps inaccurately — as having spoken of breaking the 'last link' that bound Ireland to England. More ominously, as far as moderate land reform opinion at home was concerned, Parnell even became identified with a scheme for settling some of the surplus Western population on Eastern grasslands. This seemed to presage an alliance between Parnell and agrarian extremism at home.

In two months in the USA Parnell visited sixty-two cities and spoke alongside innumerable local worthies. He also made a major speech before the House of Representatives. For the first time people began to call him the 'uncrowned King of Ireland'.

2

The announcement of the general election of April 1880 brought Parnell's labours in America to an abrupt end. He quickly hurried home. Overall the election saw the triumph of Gladstone's Liberal Party over the Conservative government. Parnell achieved the personal triumph of being returned for three seats, in Cork, Mayo and Meath. However, most of the notable successes for Parnell's supporters were obtained in the province of Connaught. It was clearly revealed — as the Poor Law union contests of March [36] had presaged (Feingold, 1974, p. 132) — that the Land League was still very much a Connaught phenomenon and that while Parnell had a personal influence in the other provinces, it was still limited. On 17 May he was elected leader of the Irish Parliamentary Party, but by a mere 23 votes to 18. There were, it should be remembered, a total of 59 nominal Home Rule MPs.

Parnell emerged from the election with his support increased, but there is no sense in which we can speak of a general mandate for his policies. Even in those areas where he or his supporters were victorious, there was substantial evidence of resistance from local elites. At Enniscorthy, Co. Wexford, and Mohill, Co. Leitrim, these forces were even able to mobilise hostile mobs.

Parnell's own selection for a Cork constituency provides an illustration of this general point. The fact that the new militant leader should sit for 'rebel' Cork has seemed to require no further comment. But in fact Parnell's selection for Cork was a fraught affair. The Cork Farmers' Club set the ball rolling by declaring their dissatisfaction with the sitting MPs. However, although some members favoured Parnell on account of the 'services' he was then performing in America, the majority were less enthusiastic about these same services. The choice was therefore postponed for a week. Before the decision of the Farmers' Club was taken the Cork licensed traders met and made clear their preference for 'Nick Dan' Murphy as against Parnell. The outcome was therefore still undecided as Parnell docked in Cork on his return from America.

He was met by warmly enthusiastic crowds, a reception which must have disconcerted the smaller cliques which were trying to oppose him. Nevertheless, on 28 March the adjourned meeting of the Cork

Farmers' Club was held and they still refused to support 'the Chief'. On 31 March, however, Parnell suddenly determined to stand for the city. Even the Rev. J. O'Mahony, who had signed his nomination papers, wrote defensively that he did not thereby express agreement with the 'peculiar' views of Parnell or his claims to leadership. He need not have worried: Parnell obtained the 1,505 votes which was enough for election to the second of the two Cork City seats.[6]

Another of Parnell's victories in April 1880 occurred in Roscommon. It was, in fact, unintentional. The incident reveals much — both about the Irish leader's private disposition (as opposed to his public rhetoric) and about the mood of public opinion in, at any rate, the more radicalised regions of Ireland. Eleven years afterwards, following the divorce crisis and the 'split', it emerged in the words of Jasper Tully, the anti-Parnellite editor of the radical *Roscommon Herald,* that 'Mr Parnell, who is a landlord himself, made a secret treaty or bargain with that great landlord leader and chief, The O'Conor Don, to have him returned for this county as the representative of the tenant farmers.' The anti-Parnellite James Kilmartin revealed — and the Parnellite James J. O'Kelly did not deny — that Parnell had made a secret compact to have The O'Conor Don returned unopposed for Roscommon. O'Kelly's initial impulse was to obey Parnell on this matter, but at the last — influenced by the obvious strength of popular feeling in the area — he entered the lists.[7] O'Kelly, of course, was victorious. The incident is a curious one. It reveals the unreliability of an over-literal interpretation of Parnell's more pugnaciously nationalist platform rhetoric in this period. For when The O'Conor Don — whom he had sought to save — was defeated, Parnell was quick to claim a great triumph. Denunciations of The O'Conor Don as a 'West Briton'

and his supporters as traitors to Ireland were soon
[38] heard on his lips.

Immediately after the election Parnell gave further
proof of the difference between the fire-breathing
public orator and the practical politician. Probably
worried by the revolutionary implications which the
peasant proprietorship slogan had for the neo-
Fenians — though not for him — he suggested that the
'three Fs' be once again made the prime objective of
the agitation. This was not acceptable to the rest of
the Land League leadership, and Parnell promptly
dropped the idea. Instead a land conference was
called in Dublin which reaffirmed the Land League's
commitment to the total abolition of landlordism.

At this point Parnell renewed his discussions with
Andrew Kettle on the land question. Parnell found
Kettle's views soothing. Although he sought peasant
proprietorship, he also shared Parnell's ultimate
political objective. It is worth recalling Kettle's words
(1958, pp. 35–6):

I told him that the agricultural depression was so
acute that no normal remedy would be able to meet
it. . . . I said that I thought we could find a way
out of the difficulty. 'Of course,' I said, 'my plan
will at first sight look far-fetched and impracticable,
but it may prove to be otherwise.' I said, 'I have
been a close student of O'Neill Daunt and Sir
Joseph McKenna, and according to their con-
tentions we have been overtaxed to an enormous
amount, at least £100,000,000 sterling. Now we
must claim as much of that money as will let the
landlords out and the tenants in on workable terms.
By this course you will settle the Land Question
and *draw the landlords to your side on the national
question.*' [my italics] He listened very attentively
to this new view of the situation. 'McKenna', he says,

'has been pressing his case about the overtaxation of Ireland on me, but I never felt the importance of the question so much before. I must go through the matter with him the first chance I can get. Yours would be a complete course of procedure if we could follow it.'

This passage indicates clearly Parnell's own position on peasant proprietorship. His hesitations on the subject were nothing to do with any reservation about the principle. He was merely concerned that in the circumstances of the day his neo-Fenian colleagues would use the peasant proprietorship slogan to achieve an immediate national uprising of some kind. However, talking to a man like Kettle, he was greatly reassured. Here was a route to the desired end that was, in Parnell's view, decidedly non-revolutionary.

Of course, not everybody shared Parnell's sanguine hope that the issue could be lifted out of the grasp of revolutionary politicians. Edmund Dwyer Gray, editor and proprietor of the vastly influential *Freeman's Journal*, was one such sceptic. Kettle (p. 36) records an encounter with Gray, 'who jokingly asked me if I wanted only 200 million that I might as well ask for three or four hundred, as I might have some left to subsidise the newspapers'. Gray's disbelief is the clue to a very important but neglected phenomenon. It explains why even moderate nationalist opinion — let alone Irish Tories and Liberals — saw Parnell as an extremist. He seemed in their eyes to be hopelessly entangled in dangerous and speculative projects that no British government could possibly accept. Again and again in this period the *Freeman's Journal* editorials pressed home this point.

However, despite these worrying criticisms from moderate opinion, Parnell was now in a position in which he had to attempt to persuade the Irish Party to accept the Land League programme and policies which had been affirmed by the Dublin land conference. These proposals were too radical for much of the party — indeed, Parnell himself had his doubts — and they were particularly alarmed by what they saw as the ulterior motives of Fenian agrarian agitators. But Parnell made a brave effort to convince the party, falling back as so often on his most basic beliefs:

> Now there is another and greater reason why the reformers ought to strike at the root of the land evil and the system of landlordism. . . . The greatest reason why the upper and middle class — and he spoke more especially of the Protestants to which he himself belonged — had remained aloof from the national aspirations of Ireland and had refused to give them any assistance had been the institution of landlordism.[8]

This was a very personal view, and it was not a way of looking at the problem which commended itself *au fond* to the majority of Irish landlords or tenants. But on the other hand, such a theme was not politically ineffective. It was wonderfully re-assuring to the moderates in the party and the country. Surely a man — so the reasoning went — so desirous of bringing over the landlords to the national side and therefore so obviously conservative in his outlook could not agree with those militant radicals with whom he shared the Land League leadership. And at the same time these radicals themselves found it difficult to criticise anything that smacked of their ideal of non-sectarian nationalism.

But the fact that his views were so individualistic was also Parnell's weakness. He could not mobilise substantial forces behind his own ideals and objectives. He had to go with one faction or another; and in late

April and May 1880 he seemed to show every sign of wanting to go with the party moderates rather than the League militants.

Whether such an inclination would have borne fruit is hard to judge, for events in the summer of 1880 were to make Parnell's drift towards moderation in the spring completely irrelevant. The Land League which had had some difficulty in maintaining itself even in its stronghold, Connaught, was suddenly transformed — by the agency of the British parliament's clumsiness — into a nation-wide movement. In August 1880 the House of Lords seemed to set its face against even mild reform by rejecting a very moderate Compensation for Disturbance Bill. Ireland prepared for a turbulent winter. The scene was set for the League's expansion into the more prosperous regions of Leinster and Munster.

3

In the midst of all this, Parnell began his fateful liaison with the wife of a somewhat 'Whiggish' member of the Home Rule Party, Captain William Henry O'Shea. Katharine O'Shea and her husband had been effectively living apart since 1875, and there is no doubt that she set her cap at Parnell. He was at that moment a considerable catch. The thirty-five-year-old Englishwoman seems to have made an immediate impression. She has romantically recorded their first meeting in July 1880:

> In leaning forward to say good-bye a rose I was wearing in my bodice fell out on my skirt. He picked it up and touching it lightly with his lips placed it in his button-hole. This rose I found long years afterwards done up in an envelope, with my name and the date, among his most private papers, and when he died I laid it upon his heart.

By 17 October Parnell was writing to Katharine as [42] 'My dearest love'.

At about this time or shortly after a Walsall solicitor, W. H. Duignan, asked Parnell why 'he did not get married, and his reply was, "I am married — to my Country and can best serve as I am."' Duignan added: 'Ireland may say to him as Hamlet said to Horatio: "Give me the man that is *not passion's slave*, and I will wear him in my heart's core — ay, in my heart of hearts — as I do thee." '[9] The irony of Duignan's eulogy, which was published in 1886 when Parnell's power was at its height, requires no stress. Even many of Parnell's most sympathetic supporters were to find it hard to forgive the liaison with Mrs O'Shea. It seemed to put a great political cause at the mercy of that lady's unscrupulous husband. All the historian can do is to reconstruct Parnell's view of the situation. The O'Shea affair revealed Parnell's indifference to the social and sexual *mores* of his day; however, if he had not been so indifferent — so much his own man in this sense — he would not have been the leader of Irish nationalism in the first place.

In Parnell's view the lady in question had been deserted by her husband for several years. The O'Shea marriage was a fiction. On the other hand, Parnell as a lonely, sensitive man who hated 'social life' found himself in the midst of a storm of greater proportions than he could possibly have expected when he entered politics. Augustus Moore, who lived in the same house in Keppel Street, recorded Parnell returning — armed with a pistol — from bitter parliamentary conflicts and then seeking relaxation from the stresses of the day by playing with a boy's train set. It is not surprising that the train set soon gave way as an attraction before the comfort which the charming Mrs O'Shea made available for him at her home at Eltham in Kent. Rarely has an illicit liaison been more domesticated. Katharine was an intelligent and persuasive woman. She provided [43] Parnell with an open affection which his immediate family often seems to have denied him. She too was well satisfied: 'For a woman of my temperament Parnell was the ideal lover,' she later told reporters.[10]

Did O'Shea know of his wife's liaison which was a subject of gossip in London political circles from 1881? In an able series of letters he later denied that he had firm knowledge of his wife's *affaire*. But it is unlikely that he was telling the truth. In 1881 the two men almost came to the point of fighting a duel. By 1882 Parnell had had a cricket pitch laid out at Eltham. He was soon to establish a study and a laboratory there so that he could continue to practise his favourite hobby. As Katharine herself said in an interview with Henry Harrison after the publication of her memoirs, 'Did Captain O'Shea know? Of course he knew. . . . There was no bargain; there were no discussions; people do not talk of such things. But he knew, and he actually encouraged me in it at times.' (Harrison, 1931, p. 123) In short, Captain O'Shea calculated that Parnell's relationship with his wife might issue in some political advancement for himself.

From this point on, Mrs O'Shea became a vital part in Parnell's life and political career. 'My own wifie', 'My own darling Queenie', as Parnell called her, became not just his companion but also an important political intermediary. Often she carried Parnell's missives to prominent British politicians, of whom at least some were aware of her true status in his life. But above all, she made a home for a man who — sometime in 1882, it would appear — definitively tired of the agrarian agitator's life. As F. H. O'Donnell (1910, I, p. 456) wryly put it: 'His business address was Kill Sassenach, Ballyslaughter, Ireland; but his tastes were in the little villa at Eltham, Kent.'

[44] However, in the early weeks and months the O'Shea liaison was of little political importance. Much more significant was the fact that in the autumn and winter of 1880 Parnell effectively ceased to act as a restraining force on the land agitation. He made no effort to keep the brake on. (This should not, of course, be confused with any suggestion that Parnell condoned violence.) He pursued the stated objectives of the campaign with maximum vigour. He had in truth little enough option but to be swept along and to accept also the fact that the somewhat stronger farmers of the South and East were now part of a truly national movement.

His role as 'the Chief' remained important, of course, but he was a catalyst rather than a purposeful or well-informed leader. He refused to be drawn on discussions of the technicalities of land reform. Partly, at least, this was because he did not have any great competence in such matters. But there was also a deeper and more profound reason. There are times when a political leader must accept that he cannot direct or shape an agitation; the turbulent latter half of 1880 in Ireland was one such time. As tens of thousands of tenants flooded into the Land League ranks Parnell flirted more and more openly with radical schemes to establish a peasant proprietary and abolish the institution of landlordism.

This did not mean that he had reneged on his personal desire to bring the younger and more progressive Irish landlords into the Home Rule movement so as to give it sufficient cachet to sway British legislators. At New Ross, Co. Wexford, in late September 1880 he stated his arguments with the usual force:

> We seek as Irish Nationalists for a settlement of the land question which shall ever be permanent,

which shall forever put an end to the war of classes which unhappily has existed in this country — and which supplies in the words in the resolution 'the strongest inducement to Irish landlords to uphold the system of English misrule' which has placed these landlords in Ireland.

And looking forward to the future of our country, we wish to avoid all elements of antagonism between classes. I am willing to have a struggle between classes in Ireland, a struggle that shall be short, sharp and decisive (hear, hear *and cheers*), once and for all (*cheers*) but I am not willing that this struggle should be perpetuated at intervals when these periodic revaluations of the holdings of the tenants would come under a system of what is called fixity of tenure at valued rents.

And now, in conclusion, I would say one word to you. I would entreat every tenant farmer not to look at the land question from a selfish point of view. You have today the first real opportunity you ever had of settling it, and believe me that when the land question has been finally settled, we should be in a position to claim with irresistible force the restoration of our old Parliament (*cheers*). Some well-meaning men are saying today: Don't continue this agitation — don't continue this movement. You are driving the landlords out of the national ranks (*laughter*). I should like to know when the landlords since the Union were in the national ranks (never). It is nonsense to expect them to be in the national ranks when they know their only hope of maintaining their right to commit wrong lies in the maintenance of English power in Ireland (*cheers*); I tell you that the best way of bringing [these] men there [the national ranks] is to take from them the right to do wrong —

to destroy the system of landlordism which was planted here by England in order that she might divide Ireland's sons among themselves — to maintain her power.[11]

It is all here. The privileged position of Irish land-lords had kept them for the most part outside nationalist ranks. The way to bring them into nationalist politics was not to drop the land agitation, but to force it to a successful conclusion. Preferably that conclusion was the establishment of a peasant proprietary in Ireland. Such a settlement prepared the way for a new patriotic unity of all the Irish social classes. It also opened up the prospect of perpetual social peace.

It was a stirring argument. Whether all the subtleties were grasped by his enthusiastic audience of 20,000 people is, of course, debatable. But there is nothing inherently absurd in Parnell's view.

The weak points are, of course, apparent. Parnell's theory totally neglected the role of the British political parties, in particular the Conservatives. Nevertheless, Parnell did not fail to achieve a response of some sort in Irish landlord ranks. They rejected Parnell's nationalism as a sentimental irrelevance, but they felt that they might benefit by his project of forcing the British Treasury to finance an Irish land reform. Paradoxical as it may seem, the landlord writer Standish James O'Grady (not to be confused with his cousin, Standish Hayes O'Grady, the eminent Celtic scholar), in *The Crisis in Ireland* (1881), a pamphlet addressed to his fellow-landlords, spoke of a 'splendid opportunity presented to the landowners of this country during the first twelve months of the Land League agitation'. According to O'Grady, at this stage the peasantry were still ready to bargain and compromise with the landowners. 'Parnell and his powerful Irish phalanx', he was later to write, 'did not really desire to hurt the Irish landlords but to help Irish tenants, and it was nothing to them if our landlords got compensation from the Treasury.'[12] O'Grady went on to claim that 'many considerable landlords in all parts of the country' accepted that this was true. They accepted also that 'the agrarian revolution inaugurated by Parnell would have to run its course'; consequently they 'resolved to apply themselves, not to the task of resisting it but that of persuading the Imperial Conservative Party' to support generous state compensation for the expropriated 'garrison'. However, the Conservative leadership refused to be saddled with such a proposal, which would have been electorally unpopular in England. Instead the Irish landlords were urged to make a last stand. Privately contemptuous of the 'garrison', the Tories were only too happy to fight to the last Irish squire.

It was not within Parnell's power — or that of any man — to ensure that the struggle remained within the confines set for it, 'short, sharp and decisive'. The establishment of peasant proprietorship was, in fact, a somewhat protracted even if, after 1882, inevitable process. Then, of course, the process was also a bloody one — much more so than Parnell hoped, though, of course, he always had his fears. Yet there is a point that requires to be stressed. When Parnell spoke in late September 1880 outrage was not such a very important feature of the Irish agrarian agitation. The really significant increase in outrages occurred in the last three months of the year. It was in September 1880 still not unreasonable for Parnell to see outrage (as he explicitly stated later in this speech) as the product of the absence of a Land League organisation rather than its presence. We cannot therefore say that Parnell's credo was a political fantasy designed to exorcise his own fears about the violence of the movement he was leading.

But there was an obdurate Ireland which existed quite independently of Parnell's aspirations. Part of the reality of this Ireland was increasing agrarian crime. Nearly 1,700 of the 2,590 agrarian outrages of 1880 (including threatening letters) were committed in the last three months of the year. Of course, most of this crime took place in the most deprived areas of the West; again, even in the West, and more so in the rest of the country, legal methods of rent resistance were more important to Land League success than crime. Nevertheless, Irish landlords were bound to be frightened by the upsurge of violence, and many were in no mood to listen to blandishments from a man who appeared to be associated with it.

For Parnell's rhetoric continued to be apparently ultra-radical. In December 1880 he even spoke again as he had in America of settling some of the Western population on the Eastern grasslands. However, a few days later the necessity for such a scheme was called in question by the influential figure of Professor Baldwin, who ran the government model farm in Ireland: in the course of giving evidence before the Richmond Commission, which had been set up to inquire into the causes of agricultural distress, Baldwin argued that no migration from the West to the East was required to deal with the problem of overcrowding on the land. There was enough suitable land in the West. Parnell was quick to take the hint from the expert and after Baldwin's remarks did not again refer to a migration to the East. December 1880 seems to have marked the high point of his 'leftism'. However, his remarks never seemed to have worried the farming bourgeoisie in the South and the East in any case. The need for rhetorical excess seems to have been widely accepted.

It was a political situation which placed a premium

on ambiguity. Parnell managed to be all things to all men. His aristocratic connections reassured the stronger farmers. They refused to believe that he was being really serious when he made some of his more radical statements which seemed to threaten their interests. On the other hand, the smaller farmers and agricultural labourers were reassured by his criticisms of the graziers and his apparent special concern with their views. It would be wrong to suggest that Parnell was purely opportunist in this respect. Many years later, when the heat had gone out of the battle, Parnell was still a notable critic of the Irish grazing system and of Irish strong cattle farmers in general. He was also prepared to make personal sacrifices for the rural poor and break up some of his own grassland for their benefit (Sherlock, 1887, pp. 87–8). Nevertheless, the strong farmers were right in their belief that Parnell simply did not have the stomach for the social strife implied by some of his more 'root and branch' projects.

5

By the turn of the year the Land League was established as the national organisation of the mass of the tenantry. Most of the Irish peasantry seemed to be determined not to pay the landlords their due rents. As this became more and more clear in the autumn of 1880 W. E. Forster, the Chief Secretary for Ireland, had begun to press the other members of the government to bring in coercion. Gladstone and other members of the cabinet were, however, reluctant to take this step. In September a decision *was* taken to prosecute Parnell and other leaders for conspiring to prevent the payment of rents and the taking of farms from which tenants had been evicted, for resisting the process of ejectment and generally

creating ill-will among Her Majesty's subjects. It
[50] was inevitable that no fairly empanelled Dublin
jury — as was revealed in January 1881 — would con-
vict Parnell on these charges. It was inevitable also
that the government would then attempt to introduce internment.

The coercion debates that followed in February
1881 were notable primarily because they had a
remarkable effect in helping to transform the Irish
Parliamentary Party into a specifically Parnellite
party. The Irish MPs who opposed the legislation had
no hope of ultimate success, but they fought their
corner admirably. Not only did Parnell find himself
working with more Irish representatives than ever
before, but also a new level of parliamentary unity
and combativity was attained. Irish orators who had
been unsure of their ground on the agrarian issue
found their voices wonderfully when the issue became the more general one of the constitutional
liberty of Irishmen. It was a field in which these
young men — many of them budding lawyers — were
natural experts. It was for the new young Parnellite
lieutenants an intoxicating experience in which they
decisively proved themselves. In the midst of all this
clamour Parnell himself made major attempts to
explain to British politicians the conservative ethos
that lay behind his apparently aggressive public pro-
nouncements. Not surprisingly, his efforts were
greeted with incomprehension.

The government had little choice save to respond by
introducing a significant change in parliamentary
procedure — the closure of debate. On the day
following this move, 3 February, the government
announced the arrest of the Land League's main
inspiration, Michael Davitt, and in the ensuing uproar
Parnell and thirty-five other Irish members were ex-
pelled from the House. Later this moment was pre-

sented by Davitt himself as *the* critical one. Irish passions were running very high. This was clearly the time to make the revolutionary bid for secession of the Irish Party and for an all-out 'no rent' campaign. In fact it is doubtful if the crisis ever had this potential. At this moment a majority of even the most committed militants feared to push things so far: in their view the country was not sufficiently ripe for such drastic action. The 'hard men' had the more limited objective of sending Parnell to America to obtain more money while they tightened their grip on the home organisation, while the less committed — the avowed parliamentarians — felt that their position had been strengthened by their good showing in the coercion debate and were consequently more ready to resist 'extremism'.

The Land League executive assembled in Paris within a couple of days of Davitt's arrest to discuss their response. But for a whole week Parnell did not appear. In desperation they opened his mail, and for the first time (so it was recalled) his colleagues learned of the O'Shea liaison. However, Parnell's views, when finally made clear, were a relief to almost everyone. Parnell refused the secession option and in doing so acted in accord with his deepest convictions; at this point they were also the deepest convictions of most of his followers. He spoke instead of the value of parliamentary work and of building links with the English masses.

Andrew Kettle, perhaps the most convinced advocate of secession in this period — unlike the more realistic neo-Fenians — was bitterly disappointed. When he heard Parnell's proposals he fully agreed with Dillon's whispered aside: 'It was Kitty wrote that, Parnell never wrote a line of it.' Not without some regrets,* Parnell had made an irrevocable decision.

*In September 1891, a fortnight before his death, Parnell lunched

He had turned his back on a rapid solution of the
[52] land problem — a rapid solution which his own views
implied was strictly necessary — and effectively surrendered the initiative to Gladstone.

The British premier continued to feel that Ireland
was on the edge of social dissolution — or, to put it
another way, was about to enter a crisis which contained incalculable risks for British policy. The
obvious alternative was to attempt to split the agitation by buying off a significant section of its ad-
herents. In April 1881 he therefore introduced a bill
which provided for a fixed period of tenure at fair
rents and for free sale of the tenants' interest in the
farms. Parnell immediately recognised privately that
Gladstone had done enough. It was indeed a major
reform. It was to bring about a rent reduction of
about twenty per cent for the Irish tenantry and to
point the way towards the abolition of landlordism.
Even those peasants who regarded the 'three Fs' only
as a stop-gap reform were interested in Gladstone's
proposal for a land court to consider rents. In the
circumstances of the time it was felt that this agency
must bring about substantial reductions.

Before Gladstone's proposal became law in late
August Parnell had relatively few problems in dealing
with it. To maintain agitational feeling was the
easiest way of ensuring that amendments made the
legislation even more favourable to the Irish tenants.
However, with the passing of the act — towards
which Gladstone developed an emotional and sentimental attitude — the situation entered a new phase.

with Kettle in Dublin. Kettle (p. 97) records Parnell as having said:
'How much better would it have been had we taken your advice in
'81. It would have been all over and won long ago.' Kettle replied:
'I suppose if the land question had been settled then, you would
have most of the property people in your movement before this.'

Refusal to wind down the agitation implied the risk of imprisonment and the loss of 'moderate' support in Ireland. On the other hand, refusal to maintain the agitation would have alienated Irish-American feeling and the radical wing of the Land League.

Parnell tried to steer a middle course. At a Land League convention in September 1881 majority sentiment refused to reject the reform. The face-saving formula that the act was to be 'tested' was produced to allay the fears of the left. Also in September, and again to mollify the left, it was decided that two tenants in each district should be chosen to determine what was a fair rent for all holdings; this was a blatant attempt to usurp the powers of the Land Commission, which had been set up to operate the Land Act. And no sooner had Parnell persuaded the Land League to adopt the programme of 'testing the act' than he sent a wire to the president of the Land League of America stressing that tenants had been advised to 'rely on the old methods to reach justice' and alleging that the test cases were intended to expose the hollowness of the act. Open confrontation with Gladstone became more and more likely.

6

When the crunch finally came, it came in confusing circumstances which make it difficult to assess fully Parnell's intentions. Despite the increasingly sharp nature of his exchanges with Gladstone, it is unlikely that Parnell was actually courting arrest. William O'Brien, the editor of Parnell's newly established newspaper, *United Ireland*, who had been in close touch with the Irish leader since the summer of 1881, records his strong personal distaste for the prospect of arrest at this time. Parnell was also speaking of going abroad for a continental holiday, which he

probably intended as cover for a further stay in the
company of Mrs O'Shea. Parnell had other more
personal reasons for not wanting to be arrested. Mrs
O'Shea was at this time pregnant with his child.
Labouchere (1891) has also contributed to an understanding of Parnell's feelings at this moment. He
wrote: 'Physically he was no coward, but he had a
morbid horror of imprisonment, partly because it
interfered with his burrowing proclivities, and partly
because he thought that it would weaken the fetishism
of the Irish for him, which placed him on a higher
level than common humanity.' At the time of his
arrest he seems to have even considered for a minute
the possibility of escape. At 6 a.m. on 13 October
1881 the porter at Morrison's Hotel in Dublin, where
Parnell was staying, was called up to receive a visit
from John Mallon, the chief of the Dublin detective
division, with a warrant for the arrest of Parnell as
one 'reasonably suspected of treasonable practices'.
The porter managed to keep the detectives in the hall
while he communicated the ill news to Parnell in his
bedroom. Parnell was told that every servant in the
house would die for him, and he was also shown a
passage along the chimney-pots over which he could
easily reach the attic window of a neighbouring friendly
house. Parnell considered this idea for a moment but
finally replied: 'Thanks, no — I don't think so.' 'Kindly
bid them wait below,' he added, issuing his order to
the detectives, according to one account, 'with a
hauteur of which his own servants never knew a trace'.

Parnell was certainly very angry. He succeeded in
cowing those who had arrested him: Mallon 'veiled
his eyes deferentially'; a red-bearded fellow-detective
staggered and looked faint — so much so, in fact, that
Parnell assumed at first he had been drinking but
soon realised that it was 'emotion quite unmixed'.
Parnell's dislike of arrest burst forth again when the

prison warders tried to search him. 'How dare you!' he cried angrily. Wisely the warders did not persist in [55] their task.

But although Parnell probably did not deliberately seek arrest, there is a sense in which it was certainly welcome to him when it came on 13 October. 'Politically it is a fortunate thing for me that I have been arrested,' he wrote to Mrs O'Shea on that day, 'as the movement is breaking fast and all will be quiet in a few months, when I shall be released.'

Within a few days the government also arrested his principal lieutenants after they had vehemently denounced the government's action against their leader. The crisis deepened when the internees issued a 'no rent' manifesto which called for a universal strike against rents: a step which took the Land League close to open rebellion. As a result — and as Parnell probably hoped — the government suppressed the Land League.

Although his colleagues recorded his demeanour as calm, prison must have been an agony for Parnell. This was not because the regime was particularly harsh, but because Mrs O'Shea's condition was increasingly a nervous and alarmed one. Parnell had to keep up a constantly reassuring flow of smuggled correspondence.

However, the prospects for Parnell's public life rapidly improved as he sat in Kilmainham. He had predicted that if he was arrested, 'Captain Moonlight' would take his place. Basically this prediction was to be proved correct. In the absence of an open political organisation, secret societies increased their activities in rural Ireland. Such terrorism was spasmodic and often disorganised. For many months, from October 1881 to March 1882, Forster, the Chief Secretary and chief advocate of coercion, managed to convince his cabinet colleagues that his arrest of Parnell and the other leaders, together with the other strong measures undertaken by the Dublin Castle authorities, was bringing the crisis to an end. But by 19 March 1882 the latest depressing batch of Irish outrage figures revealed beyond doubt that victory for Forster was still a long way off. Cabinet members began to think of using Parnell as a force for order in Ireland. They also wanted to capitalise on the widespread tacit acceptance of the advantages of the 1881 Land Act which was now evident in rural Ireland.

Parnell was released on parole on 10 April 1882, having been given permission to attend his nephew Henry's funeral in Paris. On his return from the funeral he visited Mrs O'Shea who placed his dying child, Claude Sophie, born on 16 February, in his arms. This can only have increased his desire to get permanently out of prison and return to Mrs O'Shea's side. This was made very much easier by the increasing isolation within the cabinet of Forster and his policy of repression. The predicted improvement in social conditions in Ireland never seemed to be materialising. Coercion was increasingly distasteful to the Liberal Party — especially now that it did not appear to be working. Gladstone was ready to contemplate releases even if it meant the resignation of his Irish Chief Secretary, as eventually occurred on 2 May 1882.

The basis of the understanding Parnell reached with Gladstone is clear enough. It is laid out in a letter to Captain O'Shea dated 28 April 1882 which was passed on to Gladstone. The government was to release the prisoners, would deal with the question of arrears of rent in a manner satisfactory to the tenants, and would amend the Land Act of 1881 in certain ways, notably by extending the benefits of the fair-rent clauses to leaseholders — 'the flower of the Irish tenantry', in Parnell's phrase.

Parnell made it clear that if the arrears question

were settled satisfactorily, then he and his friends would be able to limit outrages and intimidation. He did not press the leaseholders' case with the same urgency. Nevertheless, he stated some years later that he had expected them to gain by legislation sometime in the course of 1882, and not in 1887 as actually happened. However, Parnell rounded off his offer with a remarkable declaration: if the Land Act were adequately amended, this would, he said, be regarded by the country as a practical settlement of the land question and would enable the Irish Party 'to co-operate cordially for the future with the Liberal Party in forwarding Liberal principles and measures of general reform'.

Although some agrarian radicals denounced the basic outlines of the compromise, it is remarkable how broad-based its support was on the Irish side, embracing even such revolutionary figures as John Devoy. In 1891 an undignified squabble broke out between Parnell and the anti-Parnellites as to who had first raised the 'white flag' from within the walls of Kilmainham. John Dillon accused Parnell, and Parnell replied that William O'Brien had been the first to weaken. But in 1882 only the last plank of the 28 April letter — when it became publicly known — was the subject of genuine controversy. Gladstone's response is noteworthy: 'He [Parnell] then proceeds to throw in his indication or promise of future co-operation with the Liberal Party. This is a *hors d'oeuvre* which we had no right to expect. . . . I cannot help feeling indebted to O'Shea.'

What is the meaning of this apparently unnecessary concession? Was it an expression of some inner essence of Parnell's politics — solid proof, in short, that he was a constitutional reformer with a limited programme? Can it perhaps even be seen as an index of a truth about the Irish Party: that it had reached a

workable and satisfactory compromise with West-
[58] minster? In reality, interpretations such as these place
too much strain on the text.

The explanation is a rather more crude one. Captain
O'Shea had seen in the situation of April 1882 some
room for personal advantage. He established himself
as an intermediary between Parnell and a member of
the government, Joseph Chamberlain. However, on
25 April 1882 Parnell attempted to replace him with
a more reliable member of his party, Justin McCarthy.
Parnell's 'terms' in his letter to McCarthy of that
date deal with the obvious agrarian questions but
contain no reference to co-operation with the Liberal
Party. On 29 April an angry O'Shea visited Parnell
who was now back in Kilmainham. They were closeted
for six hours. O'Shea, who believed that possessing
juicy titbits of inside information was the route to
power, demanded that Parnell come up with some
new offer not in the McCarthy letter. This would give
the Captain a new prestige. Chamberlain, O'Shea's
patron, was looking for a 'union' with the Parnellites,
and this was precisely what Parnell was forced to
suggest. Parnell gave it on the condition — which the
untrustworthy O'Shea broke — that the text of the
letter should be shown only to Chamberlain. But
such a statement, if leaked, as it eventually was,
could prove highly embarrassing both to the government and to Parnell. No wonder it took so long for
O'Shea to wring the compromising words out of
Parnell. It seems likely that O'Shea was only able to
get such a result by means of compulsion. O'Shea had
only one method of compelling Parnell to do anything — blackmail. O'Shea may well have given Parnell
the alternative of the exposure of his relationship with
Mrs O'Shea (Powell, 1978).

In later years, when Parnell's liaison with Mrs O'Shea
was a matter of public knowledge, and when it also

became known that the ambitious Captain had involved himself in some of the negotiations, Parnell's critics made full use of the fact that Parnell had had a personal reason for getting out of Kilmainham and had used his mistress's husband as an instrument. In fact the careerist O'Shea inserted himself into the negotiation process rather against the wishes of Parnell, who had already made clear his preference for Justin McCarthy as an intermediary.

However, despite O'Shea's murky role in the affair, there can be no question that the 'Kilmainham Treaty' had all the appearance of being a success. On 2 May Forster, the Chief Secretary, resigned, and this more than anything else seemed to create a mood of optimism on both sides. On 4 May Gladstone, to the surprise of many, appointed Lord Frederick Cavendish in Forster's place. On 5 May Cavendish crossed to Dublin. On 6 May Cavendish, along with his permanent Under-Secretary, Thomas Burke, was stabbed to death in Phoenix Park.

The appalling crime wrecked the emerging Parnell—Gladstone consensus. It was impossible to minimise the damage. Parnell later claimed that 'if my projects had not been interfered with by the terrible tragedy of the Phoenix Park'[13] he would have obtained major benefits for Ireland. There is no reason to doubt him. The murders led to the passing of the crimes bill which Forster had prepared before he left office; had it not been for the murders, that particular crimes bill — an extremely severe one — would not have been introduced (R. B. O'Brien, 1898, II, p. 132).

Ireland now faced rigorous coercion again. The Irish leaseholders had to wait five long years before they were brought within the ambit of the 1881 land reform. It is incorrect to suggest, as Michael Davitt did, that the 'cyclonic sensation' of the murders rescued Parnell from the perils implicit in the com-

pact with Gladstone. Perils there certainly were —
[60] thanks largely to Captain O'Shea — but the advantages
would have far outweighed them.

Forster, however, was to have one last bite at the
Parnell cherry. A fortnight after his resignation he
was to force Parnell's *hors d'oeuvre* on the attention
of a stunned House of Commons. Parnell, unsurprisingly, had attempted to suppress this offer to
Gladstone, but Forster, equally unsurprisingly,
refused to let him off the hook. Parnell — unusually
for him — was visibly shaken. T. P. O'Connor (1891,
p. 221) thought that his private problems partly
explained this: 'He was profoundly depressed by the
Phoenix Park assassination, but I also think that he
was weakened by the then unfamiliar sense of the risk
he was running of shame and exposure.' Parnell
certainly had been depressed by the crime. His own
reaction to the murders had been one of almost un-
controllable revulsion. He considered retiring from
politics, but the advice of Gladstone and others was
opposed to this course. Instead he remained in politics
but began to develop Irish nationalism on a more conservative basis. This new impulse was to be embodied
in a new organisation.

7

National conditions were certainly ripe for such a
development. There was a widespread resentment
against extremist violence. The series of bomb and
dynamite outrages in English cities during 1883 and
1884, planned by Irish-Americans, did nothing to
minimise the feeling. It has been argued that this
new atmosphere merely allowed Parnell to reveal
what he had always sought. This is only partly the
truth. It is certainly true that he was tired of a mass
movement which — in a moment of exasperation —

he described to Mrs O'Shea as hollow and wanting in solidarity. But it is also true that Irish militants in the separatist tradition, either by their violence or, less obviously, by their non-co-operation, had pushed Parnell in a particular direction: that of a rapprochement with the Catholic clergy, who, under the rules of the new organisation, to be named the Irish National League, were given a voice in the selection of MPs. It is not the case that such an association, however politically necessary it may have been, reflected the essence of Parnell's aspirations.

The banning of the Land League in October 1881 made the setting up of a new body of the Irish National League type foreseeable. Nevertheless, Parnell showed hesitation before consenting to its inauguration in Dublin in October 1882. His caution was due to the possibility that the new organisation might disrupt the 'Kilmainham Treaty'. Consequently every effort was made to stress its constitutional and legal character. It was closely tied in with the political party, and its objectives were primarily *national* rather than *agrarian*. It was intended to integrate the entire population, not just the farmers. Despite appearances to the contrary, the organisation was to have a small centralised leadership. The central council of the Irish National League was in theory to have been composed of sixteen MPs and thirty-two representatives — one from each Irish county. Instead the INL was in practice controlled by a three-man executive whose powers were never defined. Timothy Harrington became general secretary — a post to which the rules made no reference! The development of the League was essentially Harrington's task, which he carried out in such a manner as to leave little room for local initiative. Decisions on the most trivial matters were often referred to Harrington.

For all the fact that it was an over-centralised,

hierarchical body, there is no doubt that the National
[62] League played a major role in the widening and deepening of modern Irish national consciousness. It was soon to be faced with an important test in this regard.

It became known early in 1883 that Parnell was in financial difficulties and that his Co. Wicklow estates were heavily mortgaged. This was by no means simply on account of his involvement in the Irish cause. Parnell was in debt long before his entry into politics. However, the sentiment developed that the Irish people ought to reimburse Parnell for his troubles. By May the papal attitude of disapproval for this scheme was announced. The result was the opposite of that intended. Subscriptions soon flooded in, key leaders of the Irish Church such as Archbishop Croke ignored the papal prohibition, and Parnell received in December a huge cheque of over £37,000 from the Lord Mayor of Dublin. The sum is a remarkable index of Parnell's personal popularity.

There was no alternative focus of popular sentiment. Michael Davitt's desertion of peasant proprietorship for the apparently faddish objective of land nationalisation substantially reduced his popularity both in Ireland and Irish-America. The result was to give Parnell the mantle of supreme realist whose leadership was the *sine qua non* of nationalist victory.

Parnell's acceptance of the cheque was rather ungracious. Such open rudeness is untypical of Parnell's behaviour. It is likely that he felt his relatively straitened circumstances keenly and that his sensitivity on this point expressed itself in a rather abrupt public attitude. But in spite of whatever embarrassment he may have suffered, he is to be found speculating some years later on the possibility of another such testimonial.

8

The struggle around the 'Parnell tribute' had confirmed that the guiding concept of the INL was the   [63]
prosecution of national ends, not exclusively agrarian
ones. However, part of the reason for its success was
the fact that the Irish leaders did not forget the land
question as is sometimes implied. The candidature
of Timothy Healy in the Monaghan by-election in June
1883 was explicitly intended in Parnell's words 'to
reopen the land question again'. The idea was to
exploit Healy's personal association with the cause of
land reform. A clause in the 1881 Land Act had been
popularly named after him. The clause which, in
Healy's words, ought to have put 'millions in the
pockets of the tenants' was stymied by a later ruling
of the Court of Appeal. With Parnell's vigorous back-
ing, Healy won a fine victory in the election. Incidentally, Parnell's zest for electoral politics seems to
have been considerable at this point. It was he who
discovered that Healy's poll had been miscounted by
one hundred votes.[14]

In other ways too the land question still played an
important role in Parnell's activities. In July 1883
Mrs O'Shea, who was now acting as a regular intermediary, passed on to Gladstone Parnell's views on
a land-reclamation scheme.[15] Almost six years earlier
Parnell had grasped the importance of this issue in
the West of Ireland. He now requested substantial
financial assistance from the Board of Works and the
Land Commission with the aim of bringing about
large-scale reclamation of land in the region. Mrs
O'Shea also passed on the page proofs of a pamphlet,
*Notes on the Congested Districts of the County Mayo
and on the Lands in the Same County Suitable for
Migration,* urging a migration within Connaught.
According to this document, there were 163,000 acres
of reclaimable land in Co. Mayo alone. The excess

population was placed at 13,000 persons. Here surely

was suitable ground for land reform.

There was great popular interest in the West in Parnell's ideas for satiating the local land hunger.[16] A land company controlled by Parnell and Baldwin bought the Kilclooney estate in Galway. In May 1885 it was announced by Parnell that he had given instructions to divide the grasslands of this estate among as many tenants as possible.[17] By the end of the decade these schemes appear to have come to little — though it was hardly Parnell's fault that the landlords always raised their prices for him* — but in the mid-1880s Parnell's apparent concern was of the utmost value in the West.

Western smallholders had not achieved their dream of a massive land redistribution arising out of the Land League. For that matter neither had the agricultural labourers. It was the already substantial farmer who made the most gains in the land war. Parnell's gesture towards the small men was therefore of some political importance: it helped to keep the nationalist coalition united behind his leadership.

Meanwhile Parnell's ties with Mrs O'Shea had strengthened. He was now an affectionate father, and for the time being he seemed to have the lady's husband under control. T. P. O'Connor (1929, I, p. 228) records a story told by J. M. Tuohy of the London office of the *Freeman*: 'Parnell took a piece of paper out of his pocket and showing it to O'Shea, asked him whether he should also supply this information. . . . O'Shea nodded an assent. It was

*This did not stop Chamberlain exploiting the issue in a speech at Coleraine, Co. Londonderry: 'But unfortunately Mr Parnell's Land Migration Company has been a dismal failure . . . and yet these men, who have completely broken down in attempts successfully to manage an enterprise which only required an investment of a few thousands of pounds . . . claim to have the privilege of governing the people of the most prosperous portion of Ireland.' (*Coleraine Constitution*, 15 Oct. 1887)

an announcement in due and rather curt form of the
birth of a daughter to Mrs O'Shea.' This must have [65]
been either Clare or Katie, born in 1883 and 1884
respectively. But in spite of the Captain's acceptance
of the situation, the O'Shea relationship was always
just beneath the surface of politics. Before long it
was to erupt dangerously.

4

'He Knew What He Wanted':
Home Rule in 1886

Of constructive faculty Parnell never showed a trace. . . .
But he knew what he wanted.

JOHN MORLEY (1905) on Parnell
at the time of the Home Rule debate

1

In the years 1883—85 a subtle shift occurred in Irish
political debate. Whereas everyone had talked of the
land question in the early 1880s, by the middle of the
decade the emphasis had switched to the national
question. This is not to say the land question dis-
appeared — far from it — but it did become subordinate
to the greater issue of Irish self-government. Labouchere (1891) has recorded a revealing exchange with
Parnell on precisely this topic:

> I once suggested to him that if the land question
> was settled, the Irish might possibly fall off in their
> efforts to attain Home Rule. 'There is no fear of
> that now,' he said. 'At first they cared more for it
> than Home Rule, but now they have grasped the
> idea of Home Rule, and the settlement of the rent
> question will not shake them in their allegiance to
> it.'

As a consequence, Parnell's dominance was due in [66] large part to objective circumstances rather than any particular personal quality. The fact was that the epoch 1883—85 in Irish history was influenced by the knowledge of the forthcoming general election. For the first time it was realistically on the political agenda to expect that the nationalist Irish — so long as they remained united — might return sufficient MPs to hold the balance of power at Westminster and thus win legislative autonomy. This prospect was further enhanced by the widening of the franchise carried out in 1884. In 1884 also a watertight pledge for Parnellite parliamentary candidates was introduced. Unlike earlier variants, the new pledge committed MPs to vote with the Irish Party and allowed them no conscientious reservations of any kind. Party discipline was thus assured; and it may be seen that the political circumstances of the day favoured not only the retention of the existing leader but also his glorification.

Parnell's position as 'the Chief' was now assured. Although this did not imply an absolute *political* ascendancy over his party he now exercised a *personal* authority which was so complete that it enabled him to dispense with most of the conventions which normally constrain political leaders in their dealings with their followers. William O'Brien was to deny that Parnell exercised a dictatorship, but even he, in the first issue of the *Cork Free Press* (11 June 1910), spoke at least once of Parnell's 'autocracy, irresponsible and more or less despotic'. He added: 'In many hearts the old Roman spirit stirred; and many brave men growled beneath their teeth even then.' It was not that Parnell himself was particularly interested in the exercise of patronage in Irish society — but it was precisely this lack of interest (and the fact that he could politically afford it) which was most irritating to his colleagues.

As a result of Parnell's charismatic dominance over his party, his personal traits and idiosyncrasies became more noticeable: the legendary frigidity of demeanour, the impenetrable reserve, the lofty detachment, the strange sphinx-like silences, the inexplicable absences, the hint of steel — all these being to some extent off-set by an engaging charm enlivened with occasional flashes of warmth and even whimsy, and his behaviour as a whole being marked by a general air of eccen-tricity. His attitude towards the rank-and-file Irish MPs was comparable to that of a feudal magnate towards his band of retainers: a curious blend of hauteur, autocracy, condescension, urbanity and benig-nity. And while he was certainly capable of treating his colleagues in an extremely cavalier fashion, they for their part seemed largely content to regard him with awe and respect and something approaching fear. A typical encounter between Parnell and a group of party members was recorded by M. J. F. McCarthy (1902, pp. 363–4), a perceptive young journalist on the staff of the *Freeman* group of news-papers:

I happened to be in the smoke-room of the House of Commons one night in company with a group of Irish members [who] ... were talking as they sat around the well-known stove. ... Mr Par-nell suddenly came in, pale, erect, self-centred; and those who were in the vicinity of the stove arose instantly to their feet. He did not address any of his colleagues, or appear to recognise them; but he took the chair which was vacated for him in front of the stove and sat down. ... He then put his hand into the tail-pocket of the morning-coat which he happened to be wearing, and pulled forth a bundle of letters. ... An awestruck silence super-vened among the members of his own party. ... If they ventured to make a remark, it was in a whisper. . . . Mr Parnell placed the letters on his lap and went through them one by one, examining the writing. . . . He selected two or three letters from the bundle. . . . He opened them and read the selected letters and then burned them. He then took the bundle of unopened letters from the top of the stove and placed them very carefully in the centre of the fire. . . . It occurred to me at the time that some of these letters might have covered remittances by cheque; but the members dared not make any comment. Having done so much, Mr Parnell . . . condescended to look around and scrutinise his neighbours. Having apparently recognised them for the first time as members of his own party, he addressed one of them . . . and said, 'Good evening, McDonald.'

Mr McDonald replied with deference, 'Good evening, sir.'

The consolidation of Parnell's dominant position within the Irish Party in the mid-1880s was accompanied by an important change in the party's external relationships. In 1885 there was sealed a 'concordat' between the Roman Catholic Church and the national movement. The Church explicitly supported the 'national claim' in exchange for constitutionalism and the party's support on the matter of Catholic educational interests. It should, however, be noted that Parnell's relations with the Catholic hierarchy were never close. The 'concordat' merely reflected the Church's acquiescence in his leadership. The Catholic clergy were authorised to participate as delegates at the county conventions to select prospective MPs. It was an ambiguous development. As J. J. O'Kelly explained to John Devoy, the republican radicals who 'stood aside' had only themselves to blame for the outcome: the increasing influence within the party of clerical and conservative forces.

The English parties were not far behind the Irish hierarchy in perceiving that Parnell's power was on the increase. They too realised that there was a clear possibility that Parnell and his party might hold the balance of power at Westminster after the next election.

The Liberals, as the party in power, were in the most difficult position. They seemed inexorably to be drawn into conflict with the Irish Party. The government felt that the state of Ireland required the renewal of the coercive legislation of 1882 which was due to lapse at the end of the 1885 parliamentary session. Parnell and his followers were bound to oppose this bitterly. As a means of mollifying the Irish, one member of the government, Joseph Chamberlain, floated what became known as the 'central board' scheme. In this project certain powers of legislation in respect of education and communications — land was originally included and then later excluded — were devolved to an Irish council or 'central board'. This was linked to a comprehensive overhaul of local government at the county level. This was clearly the most substantial attempt yet made to satisfy Irish pressure. However, it stopped a long way short of legislative independence, and Chamberlain made it clear that he feared the separatist implications of the standard Home Rule proposal. In Chamberlain's concept any legislation passed by the 'central board' would not become law until sanctioned by parliament.

Unfortunately Chamberlain miscalculated Parnell's response to his proposals. He was probably over-impressed by the Irish hierarchy's interest in his scheme. He was certainly misled by this intermediary — Captain O'Shea had again inserted himself in this role — who had implied that Parnell would accept the scheme as a

final settlement. There was, in point of fact, no possi-
[70] bility of Parnell so doing.

At the very moment when Parnell was privately
perusing Chamberlain's proposals he gave a public
indication of where he stood. At a speech in Cork on
21 January 1885 Parnell uttered his most famous
words:

> We cannot ask for less than the restitution of
> Grattan's Parliament. . . . We cannot under the
> British constitution ask for more than the restitu-
> tion of Grattan's Parliament, but no man has the
> right to fix the boundary to the march of a nation.
> No man has a right to say to his country: 'Thus
> far shalt thou go and no further,' and we have
> never attempted to fix the *ne plus ultra* to the pro-
> gress of Ireland's nationhood, and we never shall.[1]

It is a speech which still arouses emotion. St John
Ervine (1925, p. 219) observed:

> The sentiment has been used by every crack-
> brained revolutionary who has flourished in Ireland
> since Parnell's death, but it may be enough to say
> that if Parnell had lived to be the first Prime Minis-
> ter of Ireland, he would have clapped nearly all
> who make oratorical capital out of his famous
> passage into Kilmainham. It is one of those passages
> which appear to mean a great deal, but mean, in
> fact, very little.

It is certainly fair to say that Parnell would have been
embarrassed by the fact that the speech was later
used to justify the most exaggerated forms of nationalism.

At the time the speech had a rather more limited
function. To fully grasp its meaning, we have to ask
exactly what Parnell understood by 'Grattan's Parliament'. Parnell's message — hardly historically accur-

ate — was to claim that in the Grattan epoch (1782– 1800) Irish legislative independence had meant genuine independence. Grattan's Parliament, he claimed, quite without accuracy, 'had a constitution which would have enabled it to remedy all its own defects. . . . It had power over itself, over its own formation and future, as well as the future of Ireland.' The purpose of all this is clear: Parnell was marking out his maximum demand before the opening of the negotiating season. His terms would have to come down, and he knew it. Katharine O'Shea (1914, II, pp. 240–1) twigged him on precisely this point:

> When I would point out in friendly malice that his 'nationalism' of one year need not necessarily be that of another and could very easily be less comprehensive, he would answer with smiling scorn, 'That only means that lack of judgement is righted by growth in understanding.'

Certainly for Parnell — whatever the effect of his words — the nation was never an imperative which overrode other broader humanitarian considerations.

Chamberlain's scheme floundered not only on the rock of Parnell's opposition but also as a consequence of opposition within the Liberal cabinet, which eventually decided to introduce coercion without any remedial Irish legislation. Chamberlain and his Radical allies resigned before the end of May 1885. The government continued to be torn by foreign and domestic issues, as well as by the Irish question. On 8 June 1885 it was defeated by a combination of Tories and Parnellites.

2

Parnell's action at this juncture was typical. His Westminster strength lay in his freedom of manoeuvre. His duty was to pursue the interests of his electorate, and while in a general way this was perhaps best pursued by association with the Liberals, there were exceptions to this rule. In the summer of 1885 such an exceptional situation clearly existed. The Liberals had committed themselves to introducing a further measure of repression in Ireland. Meanwhile Parnell had received a strong hint from Lord Randolph Churchill that a Conservative ministry might not consider it necessary to renew coercion. And with a general election only a few months off, a caretaker minority Conservative government might also be prevailed upon to do something for Ireland.

This indeed proved to be the case. The Conservatives not only dropped coercion, but they also passed the Ashbourne Act, which was a useful step in the creation of a peasant proprietary in Ireland. Parnell must have been well satisfied.

However, Parnell's rapport with Conservative views on the Irish land question was not a startling development — leading Liberals had noted it many times — the whole situation turned on whether a deeper accommodation on Irish self-government could be reached. And here the appointment of the Earl of Carnarvon as Lord Lieutenant of Ireland with a seat in the cabinet was significant. Carnarvon was known to be sympathetic to the notion of Home Rule.

With the consent of the new Conservative premier, Lord Salisbury, a secret meeting was arranged between Parnell and Carvarvon. They seem to have been mutually impressed. It is much more important to note, though, that the vast majority of Tories were not prepared to go as far as Carnarvon. The Tory leadership as a whole seems to have been anxious to keep Parnell as sympathetic to their side for as long as possible for largely opportunist reasons.

It soon appeared as if this tactic had achieved ex-

cellent results. On the eve of the general election on
21 November 1885, having failed to draw Gladstone
into the bidding for Irish support, Parnell took the
step of issuing a manifesto advising the Irish voters in
Britain to vote against the Liberals. It has often been
argued that Parnell committed a major tactical error
in this instance. His intervention, it is claimed, deprived the Liberals of just that amount of support
which would have enabled them to pass a satisfactory
measure of Home Rule. In fact such an assessment of
Parnell's policy is too harsh. Parnell must have assumed that the closer the totals of the two main
parties, the greater his own influence. Certainly it is
simplistic to assume that a Liberal landslide in 1885
would have guaranteed Home Rule. (A Liberal landslide in 1906 was brutally to expose this illusion.)
The reality at the time of the election in 1885 was
that neither majority party accepted the principle of
a Dublin parliament. However, even if a convincing
defence of Parnell can be offered, it should not ob-
scure the element of wishful thinking in his strategy.
If anything, Parnell felt, the Tories were more likely to
deliver. He placed too much reliance on the sympathetic
views of Carnarvon and — at this time — Lord Randolph
Churchill. He did not adequately analyse the balance
of forces within the Conservative Party as a whole.

There can be little doubt that this failure of Parnell's was not a mere accident. His myopia arose out
of an obsession with a 'conservative' settlement con-
ceived in the broadest terms: the settlement that
most ensured social peace and industrial development in Ireland, achieved by an arrangement with the
English Conservative Party. As the English Radical
MP Labouchere (1891) put it, 'Home Rule apart, he
was himself a Tory.' Parnell's broad conception was
revealed in a conversation recorded by Kettle (1958,
pp. 63—4):

'You were at Arklow yesterday,' I said, 'opening the quarry and selling the stones to the Corporation, but what was the meaning of your strange speech on protection and Irish industries? Are you going to break with the Free Traders?' 'Yes,' he said, 'we have a rather big project on hands.' He then explained the meeting with Lord Carnarvon and the project of Aristocratic Home Rule, with the colonial right to protect our industries against English manufacture. I seemed to be knocked dumb, as I really was, by the unexpected news, and he went on to explain that it was not from a motive of justice or generosity that the Conservative Party were making the proposals. Inspired chiefly by Lord Randolph Churchill, the classes in Britain were afraid that if the Irish democratic propaganda were to continue, in conjunction with the English Radicals, class rule might be overturned altogether. So to save themselves they are going to set up a class conservative government in Ireland, with the aid and consent of the Irish democracy, or in other words with our assistance, having no connection with England but the link of the Crown and an Imperial contribution to be regulated by circumstances.

What is revealed here is that though we can defend the Conservative—Parnellite alliance of 1885 purely in terms of calculations concerning the balance of power at Westminster, it had a very much deeper significance for Parnell. It was his old dream of a 'class conservative government' in Ireland which inspired him: a government dominated by the forces of respectability and an ethos of Toryism.

In general terms, the Parnellites fought the election on an aggressive but perfectly legitimate constitutionalist programme. Home Rule meant a parliament in

Dublin, though it did not mean a complete separation from Britain, or a separate army, navy and foreign service; but that was all that was known, except that the Irish would try to obtain for their parliament as many powers as possible, including, as far as Parnell was concerned, trade protection.

Of course, there was always room for the occasional suitably vague rhetorical flourish. It is worth noting that at a meeting in Liverpool during the election campaign Parnell had been careful — though only after the reporters had left — to give his supporters a tangy hint of his old militancy which, as William O'Malley (1891) recalled, 'electrified and even astonished his audience':

> With a firm, set face and flashing eyes, and a voice trembling with passion, he said: 'Ireland has been knocking at the English door long enough with kid gloves, and now she will knock with a *mailed hand.*'
> Here Mr Parnell moved his arm as if knocking, and the effect upon the vast meeting was most extraordinary. It rose, shouted and cheered for several minutes after Mr Parnell resumed his seat.

But this sort of gesture remained very much in the background.

In Ireland the expected electoral triumph was achieved. Parnell won every seat outside eastern Ulster and the University of Dublin. He now had eighty-six MPs at his back 'pledged' to 'sit, act and vote' with the party and to resign if a majority of the party felt that obligations had not been fulfilled. In terms of actual votes cast, for Home Rule and against, the result was perhaps less stunning. Nevertheless, the electoral map of Ireland now seemed to show an almost complete Parnellite dominance.

For the first time the majority of the Irish electors
[76] had clearly declared for Home Rule. Parnell was in an
exceptionally strong moral position. But what was
the reaction of the leadership of the two main British
parties? To put it briefly, the Conservatives turned
against the Irish, while the Liberals moved towards
them.

The overall result of the election could hardly have
suited the Irish purpose better. Outside Ireland the
Liberals won eighty-six seats more than the Conservatives, but since eighty-six was also the number of Parnellite MPs, the Nationalists now held the balance of
power. The consequences were soon apparent. The
Conservatives realised that Parnell's delivery of the
Irish vote in England — which Chamberlain estimated
as giving them twenty-five seats — had not given them
a majority. They were quick to end the flirtation with
Parnell. Lord Salisbury's government announced to
the new parliament in January 1886 that a return to
coercion in Ireland was in prospect. Combining with
the Liberals, Parnell immediately threw them out of
office.

Meanwhile Gladstone's son, Herbert, had in December 1885 (after the election was over but before parliament had met) flown the famous 'Hawarden kite':
a press declaration by Herbert that his father was
moving towards Home Rule. But beyond this, Gladstone's precise strategy was shrouded in mystery. By
28 January 1886 Lord Salisbury's government had
resigned; on 1 February Gladstone saw the Queen,
accepted prime ministerial office for the third time
and explained his intention of introducing a Home
Rule measure. On 4 February he made a public statement which was perceived to be a commitment to
some form of autonomy for Ireland. A Liberal government, depending on the votes of Parnell's parliamen-

tary party, and generally believed to be intending a
measure of Home Rule, was now in office.

The reasons for Gladstone's 'conversion' to Home
Rule are clear. During the agrarian crisis of 1879—82
he had persistently overestimated the potential of the
'Liberal centre' in Ireland. (In this respect he was
more naïve than his cabinet colleagues, notably W. E.
Forster.) By 1882 Gladstone had realised that his
hopes were misplaced and his disappointment was
consequently all the greater. Even before the Nationalist landslide of 1885 he dismissed Irish Liberalism
(R. B. O'Brien, 1898, II, p. 104). By implication,
Parnell was clearly the man to talk to about the social
and political condition of Ireland. By January 1886
Gladstone was openly discussing the need to open up
lines of communication to Parnell. It was at this
propitious moment for the Irish leader that a remarkable episode occurred which threatened to impair
fatally the unity of his party both in parliament
and in the country. For Parnell announced his intention to support Captain O'Shea as an 'unpledged'
parliamentary candidate for the vacant seat of Galway City. For the first time Parnell's liaison with Mrs
O'Shea appeared to have forced its way onto the
political stage. Why did Parnell act as he did? The
implication must be that O'Shea was again black-
mailing Parnell and that the threat of exposure was
responsible for Parnell's dictatorial action. As Joseph
Biggar said at the time, 'The candidate's wife is Parnell's mistress and there is nothing more to be said.'

But there was a price to be paid. In the course of
riding roughshod over opposition, he publicly put
down one of his lieutenants, Tim Healy, and dis-
oriented the two most significant ones, John Dillon
and William O'Brien. In short, Galway was a har-
binger of the fatal crisis to come. Such a price was
only justifiable on the assumption that Parnell's

leadership was an absolute necessity. This indeed
[78] seems to have been accepted by Parnell and his party,
with only Biggar in opposition. Just as Parnell's greatest contribution to Irish nationalism had been to
bring unity to previously divided forces, so that unity,
once established, became the greatest reason for keep-
ing him in the leadership.

Having survived the Galway crisis, Parnell was able
to return to London to study the unfolding of Gladstone's hand. It was a supreme test: Parnell was now
unchallenged as *party leader,* but how would he stand
up as a *statesman?* Gladstone's guiding concept was
to link his planned Home Rule Bill with a land bill
and thus to deal with both the political and social
questions simultaneously. The sheer magnitude and
complexity of his project has rarely been grasped.
There were an enormous number of considerations to
be taken into account. The premier had to bear in
mind the difficulties of setting up a subordinate legislature. In this area alone there was a difficult question: how to preserve the sovereignty of Westminster
and yet make Irish autonomy a worthwhile proposition? (This presented particular difficulties in the
fiscal sphere.) But he also had to think about the
future social order and peace of Ireland. He had, in
particular, to think of ways of reconciling the substantial Protestant and Unionist minority in Ireland
to the new arrangements. This in itself divided into
two parts. In the South the Protestants were a privileged minority with heavy representation in the landlord class; in the North-East they were a majority and
well represented in all the social classes, including the
tenantry. It is probably beyond the wit of any man to
produce a legislative proposal that could embrace
satisfactorily all these problem areas. It is certain that
it is impossible for him to do so when he is hindered
by the spirit of financial caution which was the hall-
mark of Gladstone's party.

Gladstone found himself the recipient of all manner of proposals on these topics. For example, Sir Charles Russell, the prominent Ulster Catholic attorney, suggested that the premier ought to link a generous land bill to the Home Rule scheme specifically to weaken the unity of the newly emergent force of Ulster Unionism, a force which was an obvious obstacle to a Home Rule settlement. Russell's idea (which was echoed in other pro-Gladstonian Ulster circles) was that the naturally Unionist Protestant tenants of the North would suppress their political objections to a Dublin parliament if offered the bribe of a generous land bill.

It is unlikely that Gladstone took this idea very seriously. It seems more likely that he saw (as did Parnell) the nub of the difficulty as lying in the plight of the Southern landlords. J. L. Hammond (1938, p. 515) has acknowledged: 'Gladstone believed that a Land Bill enabling landlords to sell was essential to his scheme. . . . The Ulster difficulty and the Ulster protests he took less seriously.' In this perspective the priority of any land bill must be to rescue the pillars of Irish respectability and social order. Indeed, one side-effect of the obsessive concern shown by Gladstone and Parnell for the fate of the landlords was an increase in the dissatisfaction felt by Ulster Unionists, many of whom were businessmen who feared that Parnell's personal espousal of trade protection might eventually lead to the loss of their imperial markets for goods and raw materials. Their indignation was forcefully expressed in a series of cogent questions posed by one of their number, J. J. Shaw (1888, p. 37):

Can anyone conceive of a greater outrage than that we should be told that the men who are good enough to govern us cannot be trusted to deal in common fairness with the Irish landlords? Is this significant hint as to the character of our future governors intended to conciliate the Irish peasant who is the backbone of Irish discontent? Or is it intended to conciliate the manufacturing and commercial classes by telling them that a government which is not fit to be trusted with the interests of the landlords is good enough to be trusted with theirs?

But such considerations do not appear to have crossed Gladstone's mind. As J. P. Loughlin (1979, p. 31) points out, he publicly argued that once the national question was solved, Irish politics would fall into the British mould of respect for property and wealth and 'the Members of Parliament in Dublin will be very different in all respects to those who represent Ireland now'. However, Gladstone's objective demanded a decent land-purchase proposal to settle the agrarian difficulty. This in turn required plenty of taxpayer's cash to support it. The premier approached the cabinet on 27 March 1886 with the suggestion that the government should use its credit up to £120 million pounds to this end. Immediately Chamberlain and G. O. Trevelyan took the opportunity to resign. Such an early split in the cabinet boded ill for the future of the bill. Perhaps as significant, a new and important theme was added to the anti-Home Rule litany — the theme of the proposal's vast associated expenses. Gladstone pressed on, however, and on 29 March he made his first public move for leave to bring in a Home Rule Bill. Very shortly afterwards, on 5 April, Gladstone and Parnell met privately for the first time; their conversation was confined mainly to the financial, and especially the fiscal, aspects of Home Rule.

There was a substantial conflict over Ireland's contribution to the imperial fund, with Parnell persistently maintaining that the fair proportion was not a four-teenth or a fifteenth but a twentieth or a twenty-first part. 'I fear I must go,' said the exhausted Gladstone at last, and as Morley led him into the passage he was heard to mutter: 'Very clever, very clever.' In the end, though, Parnell, while threatening the possibility of a last-minute revolt on the issue, agreed to give up the control of the customs.

But despite these disputes over financial matters, the thought of Parnell and Gladstone was converging on one fundamental matter: the future of the land question. Both wanted to find a way out for the Irish landlords. Speaking in Wicklow in October 1885, Parnell had warned:

> The new Democratic Parliament won't be at all so tender of the right of landlords as the last one was. . . . Would it not be a very wise thing for the Irish landlords to recognise the situation in time — to see that if they don't be reasonable they will be chucked overboard altogether?[2]

There is no doubt of Parnell's interest in conciliating the Irish landlords at this juncture. He ascertained their views, tried to meet them and, indeed, tried to get Gladstone to meet them. In a document concerning a land-purchase proposal which Mrs O'Shea passed on to Gladstone he wrote:

> A communication, the substance of which I append, has been forwarded to me by the representatives of one of the chief landlord political associations in Ireland. It is thought that if this arrangement were carried out there would remain no large body of opinion amongst the landowning class against the concession of a large measure of autonomy for Ireland, as the Protestants, other than the owners of land, are not really opposed to such concession.[3]

This document clearly reveals that Parnell was in con-
[82] tact with Irish landlord leaders. It reveals also, of
course, a rather foolish reduction of the problem of
the Protestant minority to that of the problem of the
landlord minority. But the main thing to note is
Parnell's determination to reach some workable compromise with the Irish landowners. He wanted to get
them out of their difficulties on the best possible
terms.

There seems to be little doubt that Gladstone shared
Parnell's vision of the new Ireland. He was certainly
well acquainted with Parnell's hope that landlords 'as
individuals' and people in Ireland were about to enter
an era of conciliation. As the premier expressed it,

> Yes, I believe it may be possible that even the Irish
> Nationalists may perceive that those marked out
> by leisure, wealth and station, for attention to pub-
> lic duties, and for the exercise of influence, may
> become in no small degree, the natural and effec-
> tive, and safe leaders of the people.[4]

Towards this end, the premier was prepared to break
with a lifetime of financial caution. As he wrote to
the Home Secretary, Sir William Harcourt,

> I am the last to desire any unnecessary extension
> of demands on our financial strength. I am morally
> certain that it is only by straining to the uttermost
> our financial strength (not necessarily by expendi-
> ture but as credit) on behalf of Ireland, that we can
> hope to sustain the burden of an adequate land
> measure, while without an adequate land measure
> we cannot either establish social order or face the
> question of an Irish government.[5]

In fact it was not possible to be as generous as
Gladstone at first wanted to be. The government,
which had originally discussed a scheme utilising its

credit up to £120 million pounds, eventually settled for half that sum. Nevertheless, the land bill which was announced in mid-April was undoubtedly a landlord's bill, as Gladstone explicitly stated. It laid out the basis for a transfer of land from the landlords to the tenants, but the terms of purchase undoubtedly favoured the landlord as against the tenant side. It was, moreover, entirely optional. When Gladstone revealed these facts he was greeted with Nationalist murmurs of disapproval. When Chamberlain, speaking in opposition, asked Parnell's party to signify assent to the terms of the bill he was greeted with silence. The Belfast *Northern Whig* commented:

> The terms offered to the landlords under the circumstances are generous and even more than generous. But they are not likely to be accepted by the tenants generally and certainly not by the Irish National League for whom Mr Gladstone and his colleagues are professedly legislating.[6]

However, Parnell's reaction was rather different from that of his parliamentary colleagues. While they adopted a sullen attitude to the bill and paid heed to Davitt's bitter criticisms from the wings, he was much more conciliatory. He had, of course, to tread carefully at this moment. He had to conceal the fact — as best he could — that he and Gladstone were in collusion to achieve an agreed end. He therefore criticised certain subordinate features of the Land Bill and even acknowledged the idea that the price might be too high. But there is no doubt that, whatever the superficial appearances, his support for Gladstone was firm. Consider his comments carefully: firstly, he insisted that if the Irish MPs accepted the price, albeit reluctantly, they were bound by their decision. Parnell went on:

Then another principle should be borne in mind. I do not think either the landlords on the one side, or the tenants on the other, should be too exacting. They should try to meet each other, and it is evident that a fair solution of this question on the lines laid down will materially assist to settle the question of Irish autonomy (hear, hear). I doubt very much if the Irish landlords as a rule will appreciate the attitude taken up by the Conservative Party on this question or will think very much of their chosen champions for flying in the face of the largest offer yet made to Irish landlords to enable them to extract themselves from their position. . . .

Our view is that we should not make a party question of this Bill, that we should approach it with a give-and-take line of action by giving up so much as we can, provided we do not unduly over-load the tenants (hear, hear). We think that by giving up as much as we can to the landlords we shall clear the way for the settlement of the difficult and complicated question of Irish autonomy (hear).[7]

The support from the Nationalist side for Parnell's 'we think' propositions was more than a little reluctant. But Parnell knew his party had no choice. For Gladstone's decision to link the Home Rule Bill with the Land Bill meant that they had to accept *both parts* of the package or neither. Nothing illustrates more clearly the increasing subordination of the agrarian question to the national question. The prospect of Home Rule enabled Parnell to hold the line on the Nationalist side for his own very unpopular views on land reform. He was able to imply the need for tenant sacrifices — 'giving up as much as we can to the landlords' — as part of the settlement of the national question.

But by the end of April 1886 the fluidity in the [85] political situation which only a few weeks earlier had seemed to promise so much for the Irish had ebbed away. This was not due to problems arising out of the attempt to couple land reform with a Home Rule settlement, but to the failure of the Home Rule proposal itself to mobilise enough support in prominent British political circles. By mid-May the opposition of the Radical and 'Whig' wings of the Liberal Party, led by Chamberlain and Harcourt respectively, was obviously sufficiently strong to prevent the Lower House accepting Home Rule. The House of Lords was resolutely opposed, as, of course, was Protestant Ulster. Gladstone's conversion had an enormous impact on Irish opinion all over the world, *but it cut relatively little ice in British politics.* He kept the majority of the Liberal Party behind him, but that was the extent of his achievement. On 28 May Gladstone announced that the bill, even if passed, would be withdrawn and reintroduced with important amendments. These were understood to include some form of retention of Irish MPs at Westminster for the discussion of taxation. But even this concession was not enough for the majority in opposition.

As a result, the Home Rule debate in June became largely a rhetorical exercise. The key secondary element of land reform was explicitly abandoned. This was in deference to many loyal Gladstonian Liberals who felt it was too generous to the landlords. Speeches were made largely for the record. And indeed, this is their main value: as the historical documentation of the pro- and anti-Home Rule cases. The negative case was probably best expressed by the prominent Conservative, G. J. Goschen.

Goschen's speech was a minor classic. Firstly, following the argument of A. V. Dicey's vastly influential *England's Case against Home Rule* (1886), he [86] argued that the bill fatally impaired the sovereignty of the Westminster parliament. (Dicey had gone so far as to say that complete separation of Ireland from England was in this sense less of a threat to the constitution.) There would inevitably be constant and recurring demarcation disputes about the spheres of sovereignty possessed by the Dublin and London parliaments. Goschen then referred to the likely position of Protestants under Home Rule. He admitted that the Nationalist leaders would probably do their best to combat the natural tendency of churchmen to dominate their nations. He even suggested that the Catholic clergy were not more desirous of such influence than any other church. But the fact was that the position of Protestants in Austria and Bohemia was by no means comfortable. This struck home, as Liberals were fond of citing these cases as successful examples of devolution. Already he cited ugly examples of Catholic — Belfast Catholic in fact — threats of discrimination against Protestants.

Finally, Goschen picked up the theme of agrarian violence. Unlike the majority of speakers on his side, whose speeches were laden with profoundly racist sentiments, he acknowledged that the Irish were not more innately vicious than any other people. But he insisted: 'No people with such antecedents as the Irish could be suddenly entrusted with the unexampled powers which we propose to confer on them.' Referring to agrarian crime, he went on: 'These murders are not isolated crimes committed on the spur of the moment or in the heat of passion. There must be large numbers of men who are implicated. We hear of whole bands, and no evidence can be produced against the criminals.' Disavowal of explicit racism was therefore still perfectly compatible with exploitation of the issue of Irish agrarian criminality.

Parnell spoke immediately after Goschen's bitter and destructive attack on the bill. Count Roman [87] Zubof (1891) has left us an account of the occasion:

In contrast to his [Goschen's] small figure, agitated action and hoarse voice, Mr Parnell's tall form, calm manner and strong, almost sonorous voice, came in agreeable relief and made everybody present settle in more comfortable attitudes in order to listen to him. He ignored the reasonings and arguments of the previous speaker; he seemed to imply that he had nothing to do with syllogisms. He was glad, grateful that the English people should have come to recognise that right. Apart from its high policy, it was a salutary business policy; and he warned (he used his forefinger threateningly) those members who opposed the bringing to an end of an enmity which had outlasted parties, outlived politicians, and withstood the rigor of oppression, as well as the temptation of bribery. He was listened to in deep silence; he was applauded loudly, but not vehemently, and when he sat down everyone could have seen the impression he produced was strong and lasting, both on his followers and opponents.

No doubt Zubof catches something of the mood of the House. It is, however, misleading to imply that Parnell ignored Goschen's arguments. Goschen's piercing comments went right to the heart of the matter. They simply could not be swept aside. It would in fact be an injustice to Parnell to suggest that he had no answer. He took up first of all the question of crimes. Predictably he claimed they were related to a recent increase in eviction. More significantly, Parnell made it clear that a self-governing Ireland would deal firmly with rural terrorists. Then he dealt with the problem of the supremacy of the imperial parliament. By accepting the bill, he said, the [88] Nationalists were honour bound to accept that body's ultimate sovereignty. At any rate, in the event of Nationalist infringements of the agreement, London always had the ultimate resource of force. 'You will have the real power of force in your hands, and you ought to have it.' He accepted that Goschen's reservations about the attitude of the Catholic clergy were genuine: he had spoken, Parnell said, 'very fairly in reference to this part of the question'. As a debating point he noted that Chamberlain — now a vociferous anti-Home Ruler — had been prepared in his 'central board' scheme to give control of Irish education to a body sitting in Dublin without any special provision for Irish Protestants. More importantly, however, he held out the prospect within a united Ireland of liberal Catholics and Irish Protestants uniting to curb the power of the Catholic Church. Obviously this begged the most basic question (by what means should Ireland be united?), but it is difficult to see how Parnell could have approached the question any other way. In his words,

But I do assure the right hon. gentleman that we shall settle the question of education very well amongst ourselves *(Irish cheers)* and there are very many liberal Nationalists — I call them liberal Nationalists because I take the phrase in reference to the question of education — there are many liberal Nationalists who do not share the views of the Roman Catholic Church on the question of control of education and who are very much influenced by their desire to see Ulster remain part of the Irish legislative body and sharing the responsible duties of governing Ireland by the feeling that they have with regard to this question of education; I am sure that with Ulster in the Irish legislature and with her representatives coming together there as they came here, there would not be the slightest risk, if there was agreed any such idea, on the part of the Catholic priesthood and hierarchy to use their power unfairly against the Protestants.

Parnell played down Goschen's emphasis on the anti-Protestant rhetoric of Northern Catholics. In his view Goschen had misinterpreted these incidents. On the Ulster issue, he spoke in apparently statesmanlike terms of not wanting to lose a single Irishman. Yet at the same time he made the error of apparently refusing to accept the statistical basis of Ulster's superior prosperity. In short, Parnell's reaction to nascent Ulster Unionist opposition was less than intelligent. Its numerical strength in the north-east corner of Ireland was already apparent. In general, it might be said that if Parnell's answers on sovereignty and law and order were adequate, his remarks on matters affecting the Protestant minority were anything but adequate.

The parliamentary debate on the Home Rule Bill revealed more than Parnell's strengths and weaknesses as a nationalist leader. It also revealed the widening gap between Parnell's vision of a self-governing Ireland and that of some of his principal lieutenants. We can take the example of T. P. O'Connor's speech, which is significant as T. P. — unlike for example Tim Healy's 'Bantry Boys' — was one of the most cosmopolitan of Irish MPs:

Let me make the ambitious attempt to forecast the near future of Ireland under Home Rule. . . . The landlords are not now a very widespread class in the new Irish nation. What, then, is the nation we have in Ireland? It will be a nation of small farmers — one vast widespread universal *petite bourgeoisie*. Well, Sir, we know perfectly well the main features of the *petite bourgeoisie*. The cheek bone, the hard mouth, the sunken cheek, the keen and almost cunning eye. . . . The farmer is frugal to avarice; his industry degenerates into drudgery; his wisdom into cunning; and above all things he has the hatred, the dread and the despair of the revolutionary.

This speech requires some clarification. Already in 1886 the Home Ruler T. P. O'Connor saw the Irish landlord class as merely a relic of the past. Parnell, on the other hand, dreamed and continued to dream of their re-emergence 'as individuals' in the life of the nation. No such idea appears in T. P.'s speech. The idea of an Ireland dominated by a narrow-minded, grasping rural *petite bourgeoisie* would have been deeply repugnant to Parnell — and yet how near the independent Ireland of this century has sometimes come to this fate! We may suspect that T. P. was perhaps frightening himself a bit. Certainly he was pleading a special case — in order to downplay the likelihood of separation or revolution. There is more than a little artifice in this picture. It is redolent of the studies of the French peasantry in the writings of Balzac — one of T. P.'s favourite novelists. It also reflects, as he explicitly said, the paintings of Irish farmers by Aloysius O'Kelly. It does not allow sufficiently the differentiation of the Irish peasantry. Yet for all that, it is a striking image.

Following numerous defections from his party to the new Liberal Unionist grouping, Gladstone's Home Rule Bill was defeated. This was followed rapidly by a general election in July 1886 and the return of the Conservatives to power on a 3.7 per cent swing. As an explanation for the defeat, it became a commonplace in Liberal and Home Rule ranks to insist that the British mass electorate — as opposed to the elites in politics and academic life — was largely uninterested in the Irish issue *per se* but that it could be mobilised against Home Rule on the grounds of the expense to the British taxpayer of Irish land reform. Liberal Unionists in particular exploited the issue, with Joseph Chamberlain in the van proposing a scheme for Irish land reform to be financed out of purely Irish resources — a scheme regarded in most of Ireland as equivalent to feeding a dog on its own tail (to use the bitter phrase of Jasper Tully of the *Roscommon Herald*). But there was no denying the reality of the expense issue.

Parnell personally despised this skinflint attitude. Privately he believed — as was eventually revealed in April 1890[8] — that the imperial taxpayer had a duty to assist the solution of the Irish question. It was, in the Irish leader's view, an unavoidable historical responsibility. However, for much of the period from 1886 until the split in 1890 Parnell had to appear to sympathise with Liberal parsimony. He actually went so far in early August 1886 as to present himself as the defender of the imperial taxpayer as against the rapacious claims of his own class, the Irish gentry.[9] The primacy of the Home Rule issue and the maintenance of the Liberal alliance left him with no other choice.

For Parnell this can only have been deeply frustrating. He had come close to obtaining what he felt was a good deal for the Irish landlords. Even more disastrous for his vision of an Irish society in which this group would continue to play a major role, influential leaders on his own side were actually beginning to speak of hotting up the agrarian struggle. Parnell did nothing to encourage them — indeed, in 1886 he wryly spoke of locking up Michael Davitt(!) in the event of Home Rule. Remarks of this type, as well as his general demeanour at this time, reveal that Parnell's hopes for social stability in Ireland were fading fast.

And this was not the only problem Parnell faced. After the defeat of Gladstone's original attempt to

link the Home Rule project with land reform, Parnell
was placed in a difficult position. He had come close
to a superb triumph, but he had failed. And in the
wake of his failure there remained one vital legacy
of the Home Rule crisis. The Conservatives, after a
brief flirtation with Parnell, had rejected the principle
of Irish self-government. Gladstone, on the other
hand, had accepted it, even at the cost of a large-scale
defection from his own party. The implication was
clear: Parnell's conception of his party was fatally
undermined. He had stood always for the principle
of 'independent opposition'. The Irish Party, in this
view, was to ally itself with either of the two main
parties, according to which came nearer to meeting
Irish demands. After 1886 this was no longer possible.
Home Rule could only be obtained from the Liberals,
and as a consequence the Liberal alliance was essential
to the Irish Party. Parnell was later to say that while
an *alliance* was desirable, the *fusion* which he alleged
had taken place was not. However, he was as much as
anyone inclined to accept the implications of the
Liberal alliance in the period 1886—90.

5
'The Bitterness of Party Conflict':
'Parnellism and Crime'

A Special Commission of three judges [was set up] to
inquire into the truth of a *Times* pamphlet challengingly
entitled *Parnellism and Crime*. At that moment, the
bitterness of party conflict had developed to a dismal
degree: and even customarily honourable men did not
hesitate, in their heated partisanship, to circulate mean
and disgusting slanders on political opponents.

SIR ALFRED ROBBINS,
Parnell: The Last Five Years (1926)

In his interpretation of the politics of the period [93] 1886—91 Sir Alfred Robbins lays particular emphasis on its unusually bitter tone. This was partly due to the fact that the Irish issue was a highly charged one. In itself it involved not only the issue of national identity but the question of social order and land in Ireland during the 'Great Depression'. It was also perceived by parliamentarians as fused with other major British political concerns, including the church question, foreign policy and imperialism.

But there is another aspect of the matter which requires emphasis. The outcome of the 1885—86 crisis in British politics was a severe defeat for the 'rising stars' of British politics: the Whig Lord Hartington, the Conservative Lord Randolph Churchill and the Radical Joseph Chamberlain. The established leaders of the main parties, Salisbury and Gladstone, both played the 1885—86 crisis in such a way that they consolidated their hold over their followers. But for Hartington, Churchill and Chamberlain it was a crushing blow to their leadership prospects. Not surprisingly, they focused much of their resentment on the issue and the man who had been the occasion of their setback. Home Rule was denigrated and Parnell accused of incorrigible political dishonesty. Robbins (1926, p. 36) reminds us: 'It was the maddest of all political worlds just then, and those taking very leading parts in it lost for a time their tact, their tempers, and even their taste.' He is surely right to link this with the fact that Chamberlain in particular was a 'defeated' and 'disgruntled' man. Parnell became the target of much jealous abuse. He had done what both Churchill and Chamberlain had tried but failed to do. He had achieved leadership — and unchallenged leadership at that — of a major political party. Early in his career he had correctly intuited the political stance

which most facilitated this achievement. Partly
through luck, he had achieved precisely that sort of
realignment of political forces in his own favour
which had eluded both Churchill and Chamberlain.

Parnell felt the heat intensely. This was particularly so as regards Chamberlain. Parnell regretted the
fact that, in his view, some of his followers had need-
lessly antagonised Chamberlain in 1885, but he nevertheless regarded the Birmingham leader with intense
suspicion. He saw Chamberlain's hand in the early
moves made in 1887 to link him personally with
crime. Later one of Parnell's followers, Henry Harrison,
claimed that Captain O'Shea's divorce action had
actually been instigated by his associate, Chamberlain,
with the definite objective of ruining both Parnell and
the Home Rule movement. Neither charge can be
proven. But there is a broader, less precise sense in
which the Parnellite perception of the situation is undoubtedly true. From 1886 to 1891 the gloves were
off in British politics. Unorthodox methods would
certainly be used by those who felt, rightly or wrongly,
that Parnell had been the occasion of their humiliation. The mood of bitterness dictated a series of
moves against Parnell and the use of every available
weapon. Robbins (p. 39) was correctly interpreting
the situation when he wrote: 'Eighteen hundred and
eighty-seven is a date always to be specially noted in
our political history because it saw the opening of a
dramatic series of events which, as they developed,
first shook and finally shattered the power of Parnell.'
Some might see this as imposing an undue continuity
on Parnell's last four years of political life. After all,
the Irish leader emerged from the initial attacks in
this period in an even stronger position. But in reality the intensity of emotion surrounding the Home
Rule issue, and the more general corruption in the
conduct of political debate caused by the personal

disappointments of Chamberlain in particular, provide full justification for Robbins's view. In short, Parnell was under siege.

There is a further consideration involved here. To the list of disgruntled politicians must be added the name of W. H. O'Shea. Up to 1886 he had convinced himself that he was in the running for the Chief Secretaryship of Ireland. But after this date even that incurable optimist O'Shea must have realised that a major political career was not to be his. Either Unionism or Home Rule would win out in Ireland: the days of Whig wheeler-dealers in the O'Shea mould were over. He had, of course, a more personal reason for turning against Parnell.

Until 1886 O'Shea had been prepared to exploit the Parnell connection for political advancement; yet only four months after his election at Galway he refused to vote on the second reading of the Home Rule Bill and resigned his seat. After that he could expect no further favours from Parnell. It was also clear that he had now decided that he did not put any great premium on Parnell's patronage. Parnell therefore knew that the way was open for O'Shea to pay off old scores. Only one factor restrained O'Shea: Katharine's 'Aunt Ben' was expected to leave a large sum to her niece. If Katharine was still his wife at the time of her aunt's death, O'Shea could reasonably expect to obtain this money. However, this restraining factor was not expected to operate for long: in 1886 Aunt Ben was already ninety-three.

2

Parnell must have felt that he was always at the mercy of some twist of fortune. It is not always appreciated how difficult daily life must have been for him. How did he feel, for example, when he emerged from the Eltham house one day in December 1886 to find a *Central News* reporter in the driveway? The ever present danger of exposure must have been oppressive. His behaviour became both obsessive and abstracted. He saw O'Shea's hand in every move against him. His manners towards his parliamentary colleagues deteriorated. It is from this period that many of the stories of snubs originate. The ill-kept secret of his private life dominated his thoughts and fears and left him with little inclination to turn on the charm of earlier years. Instead Parnell became more and more inaccessible. The signs of strain were visible. He exhibited a constant fear of being followed and made attempts at disguise which only served to give him a sinister appearance. 'Do not go into the East End or you will be taken for Jack the Ripper,' Labouchere advised on one occasion. Parnell continued to feel that he was being persecuted; nor was he without reason.

One anecdote related by Zubof (1891) offers an illustration of the point. It reveals how Parnell was constantly the subject of malicious rumour:

> I never could forget the amusement we derived from some of our Unionist friends at Dublin in the winter of '86, when Mr Parnell had suddenly disappeared from public notice and nobody knew of his whereabouts. One day Mr T. W. Russell, whose dsypepsia has even bittered his conscience, came in to my room with a most peculiar expression on his sepulchral countenance.
>
> What was it?
>
> He had just come from the Castle, where he had been informed on most excellent authority that Parnell was mad.
>
> Mad!
>
> Yes, mad; and in a lunatic hospital in Spain!

Gracious and merciful powers! We discussed the situation quietly; who was likely to be his successor and so forth. Healy was out of the question of course. So was Sullivan. Dillon the nominal, Sexton the practical leader of the party — that is more likely.

At all events they were in a fix, assured me the Honourable Member for South Tyrone.

I went down to the Contemporary Club and told the news to the members, all of whom became incredulous but astonished. The Tory papers in their eagerness to believe it reported it as a fact. Finally, a member of the Contemporary wrote to assure us that Mr Parnell was at the Euston Hotel recovering from gastric fever but refusing to send out any contradictions to the widespread rumour. Two months afterwards I was over in London and in the members' lobby of the House of Commons. Mr Parnell was leaning against the bar drinking a cup of beef tea and talking pleasantly to Mr Justin McCarthy. I met there Mr T. W. Russell and glancing at him tapped my forehead. He laughed but at heart felt sorry.

Such an atmosphere — as well as his own deepest convictions — must have predisposed Parnell against taking an active role in agrarian agitation. It was no surprise to him that the winter of 1886–87 saw an upsurge in the Irish land war. All the political and economic indicators pointed that day. However, he made a point of remaining aloof from the new form of agrarian class struggle, known as the Plan of Campaign. The ploy here was that dissatisfied tenants on particular estates were to combine to offer the landlord their notion of a fair rent. If this was refused, they paid him nothing; instead they contributed the proposed sum to an estate fund which would be em-

ployed for the protection of tenants in the event of
[98] landlord retaliation.

In December 1886, when the Plan of Campaign was still in its infancy, Parnell summoned William O'Brien. The two men met behind Greenwich Observatory, which was cloaked in thick fog. Parnell pointed out to O'Brien the risks involved in the Plan and suggested that he limit it to the estates where it was already in operation. Coercion of the Plan might create some bad publicity for the Conservative government, but it was far more likely that an intensive anti-rent agitation would place great strain on the Liberal—Nationalist alliance. The general drift of Parnell's remarks made it clear that, as far as he was concerned, the political objective of Home Rule was far more important than any agrarian considerations. It should be stressed that Parnell's underlying assumptions about the new phase of agrarianism were by no means unreasonable.

The Plan of Campaign was to be associated with a new and more drastic method of coercion launched by the new Chief Secretary, Salisbury's nephew, Arthur Balfour. It also occasioned the futile condemnation of the Pope and certain Irish bishops in May 1888. Nevertheless, the Plan was never anything like as important as the Land League. It was limited to a very much smaller area of the country. It seems to have appealed most to the numerically smaller group of stronger farmers (Feingold, 1974, p. 295; Jones, 1978). (If Parnell did neglect any aspect of agrarian reality in this period, it was his neglect of small farmers which was most fatal.) But in spite of its restricted area of operation, the Plan of Campaign did give John Dillon and William O'Brien a new political influence which at a crucial moment after the split they were to turn against Parnell himself. But as Parnell (or Parnellites) were then quick to point out,

Dillon had absented himself from Irish politics on health grounds in the far more trying circumstances of 1882–85, and William O'Brien had been at best slow to see the significance of the original Land League movement.

In another critical area Parnell's concession to the exigencies of the Liberal alliance was significant. This was the problem of the retention of Irish MPs at Westminster after the passing of Home Rule legislation. In 1886 he had not committed himself on this point, but he definitely leaned towards complete withdrawal. At the beginning of 1887 the Irish leader seems to have been prepared to accept a Home Rule Bill which made provision for the retention of Irish MPs provided that he retained the right to move an amendment in committee excluding them. His reasoning was that the Tories, once they saw that a Dublin parliament was inevitable, would happily vote to exclude the Irish.

Yet by the spring of 1888 Parnell had accepted the principle of the retention of Irish MPs. He seems to have felt that Liberal fears about the dissolution of the Union required this step. There was further the fact that it was increasingly clear that important Irish questions were likely to be held over after Home Rule. It was therefore reasonable to have a strong Irish force in Westminster to intervene in these areas. Parnell's change of heart on this score won him a substantial donation to the party funds from the imperial federation advocate, Cecil Rhodes, in April 1888.

It is the obvious and correct deduction from such moves that Parnell was determined to be the patron of the union of hearts and minds with the Liberals. His public utterances in this period make this clear. In this he succeeded all too well from the point of view of his ultimate political survival. By the autumn of

1887 Irish audiences reacted with impatience to
Nationalist speakers and demanded to hear the Liberal
speakers.

3

But Parnell's moderation and relative inactivity were
no protection against his enemies. They were determined to link him with the unacceptable violent face
of Irish nationalism. In the spring of 1887 the attack
came. On 18 April *The Times* published in facsimile
a letter purporting to have been written by Parnell,
seeking to excuse, under the plea of necessity, his
public condemnation of the Phoenix Park murders.
The amazing document, dated 15 May 1882, ran as
follows:

> Dear Sir,
> I am not surprised at your friend's anger but he
> and you should know that to denounce the murders
> was the only course open to us. To do that promptly
> was plainly our best policy.
> But you can tell him and all others concerned
> that though I regret the accident of Lord F. Caven-
> dish's death I cannot refuse to admit that Burke
> got no more than his deserts.
> You are at liberty to show him this, and others
> whom you can trust also, but let not my address be
> known. He can write to House of Commons.
> Yours very truly,
> Chas. S. Parnell

Parnell read *The Times* at Mrs O'Shea's breakfast
table. This gave him a few hours to compose himself
before arriving at the House of Commons. The result
was one of his most celebrated displays of non-
chalance under pressure. As Timothy Harrington,

who told him the news, recalled to Barry O'Brien (1898, II, pp. 198–9):

> I thought he would burst into some indignant exclamation, say, 'What damned scoundrels! What a vile forgery!' but not a bit of it. He put his finger on the S of the signature and said quite calmly as if it were a matter of the utmost indifference, 'I did not make an S like that since 1878.' 'My God,' I thought, 'if this is the way he is going to deal with the letter in the House, there is not an Englishman who will not believe that he wrote it.'

The Irish leader exhibited a kind of calm indignation which was peculiarly his own. 'Do you think,' he said finally to J. M. Tuohy of the *Freeman's Journal,* 'apart from any other consideration, that I would be so great a fool as to write such a letter as that at a time when the Government were seeking by every possible means to get me into their power.' (Tuohy, 1891)

Parnell's course was to issue a denial. At one o'clock in the morning of 19 April he denounced the letter as a 'villainous and bare-faced forgery . . . an audacious and unblushing fabrication'. This was accepted by his political allies but rejected by his opponents. One of his followers in the parliamentary party, J. R. Cox, reported in the *Roscommon Herald* on 23 April:

> The scene when Mr Parnell stood up to refer to the *Times* forgery was truly striking and magnificently explained the hold the man has on men's minds, even how he enchains his enemies. When the Irish leader rose, immediately there was the most dead silence, not a sound, not a voice broke the stillness, as with a scarcely suppressed passion he exposed and reprobated the infamous charges. He looked to me . . . like a lion-tamer curbing into silence and submission a kennel of mongrel curs. . . . Two

men in particular I noted because of the eager intensity with which they followed the burning words of the speaker.... They were Lord Spencer* ... and Mr Gladstone.

It seemed, however, that the real truth would never be known. The Liberals, in fact, were rather worried and perhaps less sure of their ground than this Irish report implies. Taking the advice of the somewhat unnerved Liberal politician, John Morley, Parnell did not sue. F. H. O'Donnell, however, a former colleague of Parnell's, considered himself to have been smeared by the *Times* allegations. He launched a libel action against the newspaper, though it was not to come to court until mid-1888.

It was a dangerous crisis in Parnell's career, yet Parnell's response was amazingly relaxed. In the early days, when the chance of being able to expose the forgeries seemed faint indeed, he never lost hope and maintained a serene and imperturbable calm of mind that made his friends marvel. He discussed the conspiracy with detachment as if it concerned some third party and as though he took only an academic interest in it. The Irish leader took up detective fiction with enthusiasm. Parnell was even spotted at the Lyceum Theatre watching a melodramatic crime play. It was reported that he hugely enjoyed the unmasking of the unfortunate fictional forger! It is almost as though, having lived in fear of an attack, Parnell was relieved when it actually came. He was put out of his suspense at least temporarily. There was the bonus that as the attack was based on insubstantial charges, there was every possibility of turning the enemy's flank. Moreover, Parnell had immediately jumped to the conclusion that the forger was O'Shea. What a glorious vista this supposition opened up! Not only

*Lord Lieutenant of Ireland at the time of the Phoenix Park murders.

would he crush *The Times* and the Tories, but he
would also finish off the man who was a nagging
thorn in his flesh.

A few days after the *Times* attack, Parnell dropped
out of sight by departing to Ireland. When he returned
to Westminster towards the end of May 1887 his
health had obviously deteriorated drastically. Alfred
Robbins diagnosed that he was suffering from Bright's
disease. On 21 May J. R. Cox, MP, reported in the
Roscommon Herald:

> I sadly regret to say that his haggard and almost
> emaciated appearance has given rise to the most
> serious apprehensions in the minds of his follow-
> ers. If a speedy change in his health does not en-
> sue, grave fears may be entertained for even more
> than his physical capacity to conduct the party
> during the remainder of the session.

Yet despite his physical weakness, Parnell's morale
was good. In July he delivered an address at a banquet
at the National Liberal Club in which he urged re-
straint on the Irish people. It was a significant move;
it was clear that his Irish trip had not brought him
any closer to the Plan of Campaign.

However, Parnell was not able to control events on
the ground. At Mitchelstown, Co. Cork, on 9 September 1887 the police fired on a crowd of demonstrators
and killed three of them. Such developments only
made Parnell's life more difficult. Violence in Ireland
— wherever it came from — endangered the progress of
the constitutional agitation for Home Rule. He seems
to have been driven to dissociate himself more explicitly from the Plan.

In November 1887 he broke silence and gave an
interview to the press. His coolness towards the Plan
was obvious. He had not been consulted when it
started, he claimed (probably untruthfully), and its

conduct was now entirely up to those on the spot.
The Irish nationalist press desperately tried to cover
up by stressing Parnell's general mood of opposition
to the Salisbury government; but John Dillon, one of
the two main agrarian leaders, did not deceive himself that he was carrying Parnell with him. Parnell
went on to scotch rumours that his health had improved. He cited his doctor's advice that he required
a period of recuperation. He was also careful to stress
that, as his interviewer reported, 'Mr Parnell has not
been staying at Eltham for a long time, neither is it
true that he keeps horses there or that he has been
seen riding or living in the locality.'[1] This interview
reflects all of Parnell's current anxieties. He was unsympathetic to the Plan of Campaign and yet concerned lest the Irish people believed he was malinger-
ing. More importantly, he was anxious to scout
suggestions that he was spending his time at Mrs
O'Shea's Eltham home. Particularly since the Galway
election of 1886, insinuations on this point were
always just below the surface of political life.

Parnell's explicit disavowal of social conflict in Ireland served to strengthen his position in the eyes
of the British public. On 8 May 1888 he addressed a
meeting of English Liberal sympathisers with Home
Rule at the Eighty Club in London. He dismissed as
irrelevant the recent papal rescript condemning the
Plan, while at the same time repeating his own un-
enthusiastic attitude towards it. He was making it
clear that the Liberal alliance was still the corner-
stone of his policy and that Home Rule was still his
fundamental objective. Parnell must have been well
pleased by the satisfactory reaction to his speech.

4

But there was still the nagging problem of the *Times*
allegations. In fact this problem was to be aggravated

by F. H. O'Donnell's libel suit against that newspaper
which came on in court in July 1888. O'Donnell's [105]
case failed; but worse — from Parnell's point of view
— the case was used by *The Times* to repeat the old
accusations and to add some more. *The Times,* for
example, produced a new letter, dated 9 January
1882 and supposedly from Parnell to Patrick Egan:

> Dear E,
>   What are these people waiting for? This inaction
> is inexcuseable [*sic*]. Our best men are in prison
> and nothing is being done. Let there be an end to
> this hesitency [*sic*]. You undertook to make it hot
> for old Forster and Co. Let us have some evidence
> of your power to do so. My health is good, thanks.
>   Yours very truly,
>   Chas. S. Parnell

The spelling mistakes in this letter were to provide
clues which were to lead to the unmasking of the forgery, but in the first instance the letter placed Parnell
once more on the defensive. Parnell's reaction was to
demand a Select Committee of the House of Commons to settle the matter. The Conservative government, however, was in no mood to assist him; indeed,
it gave practical aid to his enemies at *The Times*. It
established a Special Commission to investigate not
only the letters but also the list of charges made in
'Parnellism and Crime' by *The Times* against the
Nationalist movement. Behind the scenes — and here
the Parnellite suspicion of Chamberlain is fully justified — Chamberlain was pushing the government in
this direction also.

During 1888 and 1889 the Special Commission
carried out a detailed inquiry into Irish nationalist
activity. Unfortunately the historical value of this
massive investigation is greatly lessened by the fact

that it was dominated by a series of loaded questions. It tended to treat one of the greatest popular mass national movements Europe has known as a conspiracy. It was obsessed with the role of Fenian republicans behind the scenes: with the idea that they may have been the paymasters of violence and that they were a subversive controlling agent behind the open 'front' movement. At the end of its deliberations the Commission reported that the Land League leaders had promoted an agrarian agitation and that outrages had been committed in this context. However, the Commission exonerated the Land League leaders from the most serious charges of criminal association. This was inevitable following the exposure of the *Times* documents as forgeries. 'Really, between ourselves, I think it is just about what I would have said myself,' Parnell laconically observed.

For long before the Commission reached its final, rather obvious conclusion, a Dublin journalist, Richard Pigott, was revealed in February 1889 as the real author of the letter supposedly written by Parnell. Pigott's financial difficulties and general unscrupulousness — not to mention his spelling and handwriting peculiarities — were so well known that leading Home Rulers had been quick to guess his role. Parnell, however, was rather disappointed that the guilty party was not the Captain. He resolutely refused to accept Pigott's denials that O'Shea had not been involved. He tried to persuade his Liberal backers to place a detective to spy on a public house which O'Shea used for assignations. When they refused, Parnell himself took to hanging around the spot. All this came to nothing: Pigott it was, and not O'Shea.

The collapse of Pigott during his cross-examination by Parnell's counsel, Sir Charles Russell, was accompanied by scenes of ghastly farce. As even the sombre Victorian judges rolled about with laughter, the un-

fortunate forger disintegrated. His exit lines became
more and more pathetic: 'Bad as I am, I am always
true to those who trusted me. . . . I don't pretend to
be virtuous. . . . Spelling is not my strong point.'
(Robbins, p. 94) Every statement seemed to increase
the hilarity. Few men could survive such a public
humiliation. Pigott's suicide was tacitly expected on
all sides. Within a fortnight he shot himself when
being arrested in Madrid. He was the victim not alone
of his own follies but of the vicious atmosphere in
British politics in this period.

The Liberals were delighted by the turn of events.
On 8 March 1889 Parnell attended at the Eighty Club
to receive the homage of a vastly relieved Liberal
Party. He symbolised their alliance publicly by shak-
ing hands with Lord Spencer, the former Liberal Lord
Lieutenant of Ireland.

A few weeks later (30 April to 8 May) Parnell returned to give his own evidence to the Special Commission. His performance was little short of ludicrous.
He certainly misled the Commission on the question
of his connections with Fenianism in the 1870s. This
may reasonably be put down to political necessity.
Yet it is difficult to avoid the feeling that Parnell
carried this to an unnecessary extreme – and one
which was embarrassing to his followers. As Jasper
Tully later noted critically, 'Parnell gave the impression that he knew nothing about the movement
he was supposed to be leading.'[2] Yet this exaggerated terseness was combined with occasional out-
breaks of quite needless verbosity – for example, in
his unnecessary admission that he had in 1881
'deliberately misled' the House of Commons about
the existence of secret societies in Ireland. Robbins
(p. 109) noted:

> The one whom the public had agreed to regard as
> 'the strong silent' man of mythical value in the

world's affairs proved diffuse, explanatory, argumentative, everything a perfect witness should not be. Asquith [H. H. Asquith, Russell's junior counsel] soon found the difficulty. 'Are you a son of the late Mr John Parnell?' he started by asking. Instead of the simple affirmative required, Parnell gave a long biographical sketch of that deceased parent. 'Too discursive' was the note I made.

'Yes,' Parnell admitted later in the day to J. M. Tuohy, after his remark about misleading the House, 'that was an absurd answer, but the truth of it is that when I gave it I was so worn out in body and mind from standing in the box for the three days, replying to the tiresome and irritating questions of the Attorney-General, that almost any answer could have been extracted from me.' (Tuohy, 1891)

Aware of the irritation caused in Ireland by his rather poor performance, Parnell covered his tracks with a fine — and totally untypical for this period — display of oratorical militancy when accepting an address from the municipal bodies of Ireland towards the end of May. But in the final analysis Parnell's unimpressive testimony counted for little at the time. The fact that his enemies had been exposed in a dishonourable attempt to discredit him was the all-important consideration. The Unionist cause was at its lowest ebb since 1886. On 18 December 1889 the triumphant, if sickly, Parnell was received by Gladstone at Hawarden. The two leaders enjoyed a friendly discussion of the outlines of a possible measure of Irish legislative autonomy.

Parnell's ascendancy was at its height. But such unparalleled dominance was not to last long. On Christmas Eve 1889 Captain O'Shea filed a petition for divorce from his wife, citing the nationalist leader as co-respondent.

Before the O'Shea suit Parnell's supremacy was un-
questioned. Although his state of health since 1887
(it is now known that he was suffering from some
form of kidney disease) had, by his own admission,
reduced his effectiveness as a parliamentarian, there is
a sense in which Parnell's low profile was politically
functional, or at least not actually dysfunctional. In
the post-1886 period it behoved the British Liberal
Party to be in the van in making the case for Home
Rule. It was thought that it would be more politically
persuasive if the Irish took a back seat for a while as
the converts convinced others of the rationality of
their new stance. Parnell's distant attitude towards
the Plan of Campaign had had remarkably little ill
effect on his leadership. This movement was nothing
like as deeply rooted as the earlier Land League.
Dillon and O'Brien, the most actively involved of
Parnell's lieutenants, became the object of a great
deal of clerical flac and replied in kind. Parnell was
therefore able to present himself as the realistic
centrist — as in his Eighty Club speech of May 1888 —
who concentrated on the main subject, Home Rule,
while his agrarian left and his clerical right got side-
tracked on secondary issues.

It should be noted in the late 1880s the party itself
was a rather less inspiring body than in earlier years.
Frequent public references were now made to a
'plague' of opportunist lawyer MPs who displayed less
than the necessary ardour. In August 1889 the *Freeman's Journal* declared that the Irish Party was a
more effective fighting force 'when they were thirty
or forty than now when they are eighty-six'.[3]

Parnell was further assisted by the fact there was
no sign of any serious competitor for the leadership.
Certainly neither Dillon nor O'Brien had his experience. It is a fact which is often overlooked — perhaps

because of Parnell's relative youth at his death — but [110] in 1890 and 1891 Parnell could boast, despite his illness and irregular involvement, a longer consistent record of public activity in nationalist politics than any other significant parliamentarian. It is therefore no surprise to find that at the beginning of 1890 the party offered Parnell an unequivocal and laudatory statement of support. This came not simply after O'Shea had opened divorce proceedings, but also after a public statement by Parnell which revealed clearly that there was a basis to those proceedings. This came on 30 December 1889 when the *Freeman's Journal* reported a remarkable assertion: 'Captain O'Shea was always aware that he [Parnell] was constantly there [Mrs O'Shea's house at Eltham] in his absence from 1880 to 1886, and since 1886 he has known that Mr Parnell constantly resided there from 1880 to 1886.' This declaration throws a revealing light on Parnell's assurance to Michael Davitt that 'he would emerge from the whole trouble without a stain on his reputation'. Parnell seems to have meant — although Davitt did not understand him this way — that while the charge of adultery was not false, he had followed a gentleman's code of honour and that Captain O'Shea had not been deceived.

It was therefore Captain O'Shea and the divorce case alone which brought down Parnell. Nothing else at the time could have undermined his leadership. Why, then, did the Captain act as and when he did? Up to 1886 O'Shea certainly exploited the Parnell connection for political advancement; but in June 1886, four months after his election at Galway, he walked out of parliament rather than vote on the second reading of the Home Rule Bill and resigned his seat. After this development O'Shea could no longer look to Parnell for any further political help. But O'Shea still had one strong reason for inactivity. He expected his wife's aged Aunt Ben to leave a large sum to her niece. If he remained Katharine's husband, O'Shea might reasonably expect to share in this windfall. In the late 1880s the nonagenarian Aunt Ben's death was expected almost daily by the Captain.

This background information helps to explain why O'Shea acted at this juncture. Aunt Ben's death on 19 May 1889 was followed by the revelation that she had left her money to Katharine in such a way that O'Shea was not legally entitled to a share. The will was contested by Katharine's brothers and sisters as well as by O'Shea himself: this probate case placed the money out of reach for at least three years. O'Shea therefore had no further motive for silence or delay. In fact a divorce action, if successful, might have weakened Katharine's chances when it came to the matter of the will.

What was Parnell's strategy in this new crisis? Labouchere (1891) speculated that Parnell had rather too optimistic a view about the likely Irish reaction: 'One morning while the case was proceeding he sat quietly reading the report of the evidence. He calmly looked up and said, "My people never will believe all this."' Labouchere adds: 'In the end he was so eager for the divorce that he would not have prevented it had he been able.'

This seems to be the truth of the matter. Although Mrs O'Shea may perhaps have been interested in proving in court that the Captain was a conniving husband, Parnell, on the other hand, was not. He was naturally anxious that Katharine should inherit her aunt's estate – he had, after all, for years been engaging in deception and subterfuge with this end in view – but his overriding concern now was not to take any step which might endanger the prospects of outright divorce and his eventual marriage to Katharine. The future of their two children had, of course, also to be taken into consideration. At any rate it was Parnell's hope that O'Shea could be 'squared' with a sum of £20,000: in return for this substantial bribe it was hoped — reasonably enough — that the Captain might confess his own adultery with some party. However, in the end the money was unavailable and O'Shea pressed his case successfully.

It cannot be stressed enough: if O'Shea had been 'squared', Parnell would have remained the undisputed leader of his party. Instead Parnell found himself in the position of having raised hopes that he would triumph here as he had triumphed over *The Times;* with his failure to do so, it should not be surprising that an embittered reaction set in against him. Parnell was eventually destined to lose his unique position of power and authority for the want of a ready £20,000 in 1890.

6
'Sticking to His Corner'

Well, I confess that I don't admire a man who doesn't stick to his corner and fight it out whether he is losing or winning.

PARNELL, reported in
Roscommon Messenger, 3 Oct. 1891

1

The divorce case began on 15 November 1890. No defence was entered, and the trial lasted a mere two days. The evidence presented the two lovers in the most squalid light: most ludicrous of all, it was alleged that Parnell had on occasions evaded the Captain by departing rapidly down a fire-escape. A decree *nisi* was granted on 17 November. On the following day the Dublin branch of the National League passed a resolution upholding Parnell's leadership. The meet- ing of the party to elect their sessional leader, the technical title of the Irish leader, was fixed for Tuesday 25 November. Meanwhile everyone held their breath. Then events took a sudden twist.

Parnell was at the height of his power, and it was difficult for any Irish force to move against him. The bishops were silent — some explicitly declaring the issue to be purely political. (This was a fact Parnell was later to exploit in 1891 when the bishops rediscovered their capacity for moral leadership.) It was rather the 'Nonconformist conscience' in England which openly rebelled first against Parnell. The Liberal leader, Gladstone, found that a large proportion of his own supporters would no longer support an alliance with the Irish if the Irish were led by Parnell. Gladstone then sent for Justin McCarthy, generally regarded as Parnell's second-in-command, and, while paying tribute to Parnell's work, told him that Parnell's retention of the leadership would mean the loss of the next election and would mean also the putting off of Home Rule until a time when he (Gladstone) would no longer be able to lend a hand in the struggle. In order to avoid the charge of 'dictation', Gladstone had resolved not to convey this directly to Parnell himself, but he authorised McCarthy to pass on these opinions to Parnell when he next saw him. McCarthy attempted to contact Parnell, but without success or, at any rate, impact.

Gladstone also took the step of addressing a letter to Morley, incorporating his conversation with McCarthy and claiming that the continuance of Parnell's leadership

would not only place many hearty and effective friends of the Irish cause in a position of great embarrassment, but would render my retention of the leadership of the Liberal Party, based as it has been mainly upon the prosecution of the Irish cause, almost a nullity.

Gladstone further stated in this letter that he had requested McCarthy to make known his viewpoint at the meeting of the party in the event of Parnell showing no sign of retirement.

However, neither Morley nor McCarthy were able to get this point through to Parnell before the meeting of the Irish Parliamentary Party on 25 November. Parnell's famous inaccessibility once more came to his (temporary) rescue. Even more remarkably, Justin McCarthy failed to tell the other party members once the meeting had started. When all allowance is made for the possibility of a genuine misunderstanding of Gladstone's instructions on McCarthy's part, it seems clear that his nerve failed him. 'That nice old gentleman for a tea-party', as Parnell later called McCarthy, could not cope with the harsh reality of high politics.

Parnell was therefore able to make his appeal under the best possible conditions. His themes were rudimentary. He denied any friendship with O'Shea; he insisted vehemently that he had never accepted any hospitality from him; he hinted of further important disclosures which would show his position in a better light; and finally, he appealed to the collective loyalty of the party. Slightly stunned — for some members were expecting Parnell to conclude by resigning — the party unanimously re-elected him to the chair. They did so — thanks to McCarthy's pusillanimity — without the knowledge of Gladstone's assessment of the political situation.

As Parnell emerged from the meeting he met the anxious Morley. Morley took the opportunity to read out Gladstone's letter to him. In reply, Parnell refused to resign. 'Of course,' he said as he left Morley, 'Mr Gladstone will have to attack me. I shall expect that. He will have a right to do that.'

Gladstone indeed had no choice but to attack Parnell if he was to secure his own following. Rapidly the Liberal leader had the text of his letter to Morley sent to the press. The time for discreet pressure — if there was ever a time for it — had passed. Everything was now set before the public.

On the publication of the letter the members of the Irish Party were confronted with unmistakable evidence that the crisis would not just go away. Thirty-one members signed a requisition asking for a special meeting of the party. Parnell opposed this move but was overruled. This was a decisive moment: clearly the tide was beginning to turn unambiguously against him. Following this development, and further criticism in the press from Michael Davitt, Parnell attempted to go on the offensive by issuing a manifesto attacking Gladstone and a section of the Irish Party. The manifesto, which was published on 29 November under the title 'To the People of Ireland', was explicit. It stressed that a portion of the Irish Party had lost its independence. The Liberal alliance, Parnell claimed, had been desirable, but this alliance had evolved into a 'fusion'. He then attempted to make damaging revelations about his visit to Gladstone at Hawarden in December 1889, when, he said, Gladstone had confided to him the details of the Home Rule proposals which the next Liberal administration would introduce.

These included — according to Parnell — the reduction of the Irish representation in the imperial parliament from 103 to 32; reservation to the imperial parliament of power to deal with the land question; constabulary to be kept under imperial control for an indefinite period, judges for ten to twelve years.

With so much reserved to the imperial parliament, [116] Parnell was unwilling to consent to a reduction of the Irish representation at Westminster. Parnell had told Gladstone that he would try to 'reconcile Irish opinion' on the constabulary and judges, but he dissented from the reduction of the representation and from the absence of a land settlement. The feeble nature of the Liberal proposals had a definite implication. The Irish Party must retain its independence at all costs. Even if an 'independent' policy led to the defeat of the Liberals at the next general election, 'a postponement would be preferable to a compromise of our national rights by the acceptance of a measure which would not realise the aspirations of our race'.

All this, of course, was open to a damning objection. If the Liberals were so unreliable, why had Parnell himself preached the virtues of alliance in so many of his public statements in the past two years? Parnell attempted to explain this away:

> It was impossible for me to disclose by public speech or by private explanation the setback which the Hawarden communications had given to the cause of Home Rule and the perplexity with which they had filled my mind. The matter was still not definitely settled. Until all hope had been removed of arriving at a satisfactory undertaking upon these important subjects with Mr Gladstone it would have been highly improper for me in any way to have referred publicly to the matter, and it would have been difficult for me to have selected from amongst my colleagues for the purpose of a disclosure.[1]

Only a minority were to be convinced by this special pleading. Most found Gladstone's repudiation of Parnell's version of the Hawarden interview to be crushingly explicit in detail. It seems fair to conclude that Parnell mixed up certain genuine concerns (for example, the difficulties which still faced the Liberal Party in producing a sufficiently generous land reform) with other very much more tendentious suggestions. It is highly improbable that Gladstone could have tied his hands by laying down precise details concerning such controversial legislation. At best, Parnell seems to have presented items for discussion as if they were hard and fast proposals.

Following such an open breach with the Liberal Party, one thing was now clear. The cause of Home Rule was heavily damaged. The only question now was: were the other members of the Irish Party prepared to allow Parnell to continue this strategy, or would they split with him and thus divide the movement in Ireland as the price of the retention of the Liberal alliance?

2

Events turned sharply against Parnell. On 30 November a manifesto was issued by five of the six Irish MPs who happened to be in America (W. O'Brien, J. Dillon, T. P. O'Connor, T. P. Gill and T. D. Sullivan) asking the Irish Party to repudiate Parnell. Last-minute support for a change in the leadership came from Archbishops Walsh and Croke.

On 1 December the 'requisitioned' meeting of the party opened a new debate on the leadership in Committee Room Fifteen at Westminster. An early indication in the balance of forces was given when Colonel Nolan's motion to postpone the issue was defeated by 44 votes to 29. During the first two days of the lengthy debate the standard of discussion was surprisingly high. There was, however, one symptomatic moment of bitter personal conflict when Tim Healy accused Parnell of misrepresenting the interview with

Gladstone at Hawarden. 'I will not stand an accusa-
[118] tion of falsehood from Timothy Healy,' Parnell ex-
claimed angrily, and Healy was prevailed upon to
withdraw. Desperately the party tried to achieve a
compromise. It sought guarantees from Gladstone of
a satisfactory Home Rule measure if Parnell was to
retire. But Gladstone refused to be pressurised in
this way, and the party was thrown back on its own
resources. These resources — of tolerance and good-
will, at least — were wasting away in the course of the
long debate. Finally, when one of Parnell's supporters,
John Redmond, referred to 'the master of the party',
Tim Healy could not resist the malevolent quip: 'Who
is to be the mistress of the party?' Parnell bitterly
retorted by describing Healy as that 'cowardly little
scoundrel . . . who dares in an assembly of Irishmen
to insult a woman'. 'I made no reply,' Healy said
later, 'being contented with the thrust that will stick
as long as his cry about Gladstone's "dictation" con-
tinues.'

After this there was no hope of any rapprochement.
The majority of the party — 45 members, led by Justin
McCarthy — withdrew from Committee Room Fifteen,
leaving Parnell with 27 followers. Bitter words had
been spoken, words which were to have a divisive
effect in Irish politics for many years to come. Furthermore, on 3 December the Catholic hierarchy, with
the support of the majority of the priests, called on
the Catholic people of Ireland to repudiate Parnell.
Now all eyes turned to Ireland.

3

On 10 December Parnell arrived in Dublin to a hero's
welcome. He was to retain the capital's loyalty to the
end. However, while he addressed his meeting the
anti-Parnellites took the opportunity to seize Parnell's

paper, *United Ireland,* and its offices. Parnell himself
led the crowd which stormed and retook the building;
white with fury, he himself smashed in the door with
a crowbar and played a leading part in the vicious
scuffle which then took place in the entrance hall.
The violence and the excitement of the occasion seem
to have been therapeutic. He told Katharine O'Shea
later: 'It was splendid fun. I wish I could burgle my
own premises every day.' But the high jinks did not
stop his critics raising awkward questions. At this
juncture Parnell was asked by a journalist:

Q. What course will the Liberal Party be likely to
take with regard to Home Rule?
A. That is for Mr Gladstone to say. There is no
doubt that the Liberal Party is bound to Home
Rule, and cannot come into power without it.
In proportion as the independence and in-
tegrity of the Irish Party is lost, so a measure
of Home Rule is diminished, and the stronger
and more independent we remain, the larger,
better and more satisfactory will be the settlement.[2]

This, of course, was the weak spot in Parnell's case.
The Liberal Party was not irrevocably committed to
Home Rule in all circumstances; in particular, it was
not committed if the Irish leader was tainted by scan-
dal. Parnell's effort to convince the Irish on this point
was bound to fail. Few could believe that his retention of the leadership would not weaken the Home
Rule cause. Even fewer could accept Parnell's suggestion that his continued leadership would actually
ensure a better settlement.

There was a parliamentary vacancy in North Kilkenny. Parnell and his opponents vied for the constituency in a tense and bitter atmosphere. Parnell
was said to have degraded a passing funeral by

shouting out that it bore the opposing candidate's
[120] political corpse. The Parnellites replied that Parnell's
words had been addressed only to an empty hearse. The
campaign continued to be marked by incidents that
grew steadily more ugly. Davitt, who continued to
oppose Parnell, was attacked by Parnellites at the
village of Ballinakill. Parnell was hit by a bag of
lime, some of which entered his eye and caused him
extreme discomfort. On 22 December 1890, by almost
two to one, Parnell's first direct appeal to a body of
Irish electors was rejected. The sign was clear: although
Parnell had much loyal support, it was only about
one-third of the nationalist Irish.

On Christmas Day he called on Canon Dunphy, a
visit which was recollected in the *Waterford Star* on
27 April 1895:

> He was totally worn out and asked Father Dunphy
> for something to eat and drink. 'Yes,' said Father
> Dunphy, 'you will always have them from me. I
> am sorry to meet you in this way,' continued the
> Canon to Parnell, 'sorry for yourself. Where was
> your brain? Why did you not get three sensible
> men to advise you? You went through most
> stormy times and you were able to meet your
> enemies, the *Times* and the Pigottites.' To this
> Parnell replied that he was getting old like Canon
> Dunphy and would get sense, and went on, 'In less
> than three months we will be together again and
> will get the blessings of Ireland and the Archbishop
> of Cashel.'

Yet despite his setbacks, Parnell's course was one
of resolute refusal to compromise. In the early weeks
of 1891 first William O'Brien and then John Dillon,
both speaking at meetings in France, attempted to
link his withdrawal with the concession by the Liberals of the kind of guarantees about Home Rule which

Parnell himself had sought in the Committee Room Fifteen debate. It is worth noting that even at this moment of crisis Parnell was concerned about the fate of his fellow-landlords. O'Brien (1923, p. 158) has made it clear that Parnell was determined that the imperial parliament should resolve the land question before the implementation of Home Rule. Far from wanting the landlords to be at the mercy of a Dublin parliament — as Dillon was later to desire — Parnell felt that it was wrong that 'the Irish parliament [should be] loaded with so intolerable a responsibility'. But despite the fact that considerable advance was made in the business of obtaining these guarantees, Parnell broke off the negotiations. He simply could not bring himself to surrender. 'If I go, I go forever,' seems to have been his view. For a man whose appetite for politics had at times in the late 1880s seemed to be rather jaded, his desire to cling on to power — once it had been threatened — is most striking. Once Katharine pleaded with him to relent, but his reply was adamant as ever;

'I am in your hands, Queenie, and you shall do with me what you will; but you promised. . . .'

'You mean I promised that I would never make you less than —'

'Less than your King,' he interrupted, 'and if I give in now I shall be less than that. I would rather die than give in now — give in to the howling of the English mob.'

J. M. Tuohy (1891) speculated about Parnell's conduct during these negotiations:

It may have been that his uninterrupted course from victory for sixteen years had imbued a mind somewhat susceptible to occult influence with something of a fatalistic tinge, and that he had be-

come convinced that fate had appointed him its
special instrument to secure for his countrymen
the fulfilment of their aspirations. It required some
such hypothesis to account for the impassive
resolution with which he argued down all suggestions, from whatever source they proceeded, which
had for their object the real conservation of his
influence and position by bringing about his temporary retirement.

Parnell was thus launched on the final phase of the
most bitter struggle of his life. The struggle was waged
with an obscene verbal cruelty and frequent physical
violence on both sides. It was war to the knife, with
no holds barred — a mode of conflict which inevitably
told more heavily on the weaker party.

4

Two more seats fell vacant — unluckily for Parnell. In
April an election became necessary in North Sligo,
and another in Carlow in July. A victory at the polls
was vitally necessary if any popular confidence in
Parnell's leadership was to be restored. In North
Sligo, where clerical influence was exerted for as well
as against him, it seemed for a time that he might be
successful, but in the outcome his candidate was defeated by a fairly narrow margin. The result may well
have been a decisive setback in Parnell's campaign to
regain his lost ascendancy: thereafter his popularity
waned rapidly, and the result at Carlow, where his
reluctant candidate, Andrew Kettle, was heavily defeated, was for many observers a foregone conclusion. Nothing daunted, on 25 June 1891 he married
Katharine O'Shea at the registry office in Steyning
and provoked the defection from his side of the
unctuously Catholic *Freeman's Journal*. Two days later

he celebrated his forty-fifth and last birthday. In his heart he cannot have been a happy man. The experience of abuse must have been an excruciating one for a man of Parnell's disposition.

The issue of Parnell's leadership had become linked with other issues of contemporary political concern as his opponents turned for any stick with which to beat him. Divisive themes in Irish politics suddenly became prominent. Irritations that had lain dormant were no longer suppressed: there was no home truth — on either side — so frank that it could not be spoken. This gives the last year of Parnell's life a unique interest.

Increasingly Parnell's moderation on the land question was censured. In 1891 men were prepared to say — as they would never have dared in earlier years — that this was the logical result of having a landlord at the head of the Home Rule movement. Even before the split, for example in a crucial speech in parliament on 21 April 1890, Parnell had made public his reservations about party orthodoxy on the land question. He was increasingly heedless of the views of his principal supporters. Morley (1905, I, p. 245) recalled:

> In 1890 he was much exercised on land purchase. He once asked me to speak with him, having devised a very complex and impracticable set of proposals which he slowly expounded to me. I asked him would his people like it? He did not care whether they did or not, he had thought it over for ten years.

Not surprisingly, Morley adds that 'the most important of Parnell's lieutenants' were mystified by the public declaration when it came. The gist of Parnell's speech was to stress that the dimension of the Irish land question was customarily *exaggerated*. He spoke as the friend, he said, of the smaller tenantry and

middling gentry who were locked in a futile, mutually
[124] destructive conflict. (The large landed magnates, in
Parnell's view, were swallowing up the lion's share of
the government compensation so far, while the larger
farmers were notoriously unproductive.) He spoke of
limiting a land-purchase measure to tenants valued at
under £50, thus annoying a large section of the Irish
tenants, and also suggested a conspicuously low valuation of the whole province of Connaught, which
angered Conservative opinion. But after the split it
was the nationalist camp which was to denounce the
speech. Jasper Tully critically noted: 'Mr Parnell is a
landlord himself and his most notable speech in the
House of Commons was to advocate the retention of
the landlords in the country and to oppose the benefits of Land Purchase to anyone over £50 valuation.'[3]
James Daly put it even more simply: 'A landlord himself, he was never truly the enemy of landlordism.'[4]
In 1891 it was openly declared that Parnell had failed
to transcend his class origin. There is much that is
unprincipled and demagogic in these attacks. The
divorce crisis had brought Parnell down and any line
of attack was legitimate. But one point that Tully was
to make did have a certain amount of substance. By
establishing a migration company Parnell had raised
hopes in the West in 1883–84 which he had totally
failed to satisfy. Parnell's last series of public speeches
were concentrated in that region; this indicates a be-
lated awareness that this was a decisive area of struggle.
But by this time there was no hope of mobilising the
massive support he needed from the smallholders.

5

Perhaps most important of all, the ideological content
of the majority trend in Irish nationalism underwent
a significant change during Parnell's last desperate

campaign. Whereas it is true to say that the Land
League had been remarkably free of anti-urban,
narodnik or overtly sectarian Catholic sentiments, all
these themes came to the fore in the opposition to
Parnell. A new emphasis began to be given to the
claim that rural Irishmen were the only reliable
Catholics and patriots. Jasper Tully, for example,
claimed: 'Parnell says as Paris is to France so Dublin
is to Ireland. As they must take their allusions from
French history, we tell them they will meet their *La
Vendee.*' Dublin, in Tully's vision, was the 'moral
cesspool of Ireland' counterposed to 'the men of the
West and South, who love their religion and country'.[5]
Dubliners, he claimed, had given the infamous Lily
Langtry a heroine's welcome.

With this sort of rhetoric the Irish revolution had
come full circle. The young radicals of 1879 – of
whom Tully had been so conspicuous an example –
had self-consciously invoked the spirit of the secular
idealism of the French revolution of 1789. Twelve
years later they were reduced to invoking – equally
self-consciously – the French counter-revolution.

However, tough talking was not limited to the
anti-Parnellite side. Parnell too unburdened himself of
some unpalatable truths. In doing so, he performed a
lasting service for Irish politics. There is a view which
presents Parnell's last year as totally unrepresentative
of his broad contribution. In his desire to achieve his
objectives, it is said, Parnell adopted a completely unprincipled course. He went down ingloriously locked
in a maniacal paroxysm of anti-Catholicism, Fenianism and socialism. There is much superficial truth in
this observation. We can accept that Parnell owed his
first parliamentary seat to an alliance with the priests,
and although he may have occasionally tangled with
them in the 1880s, it was the grossest hypocrisy to
assault them after the divorce crisis. Again, the Parnell

of the 1880s was a firmly constitutional politician.
After 1886 he was a supporter of an alliance with the British Liberal Party. Finally, Parnell was a known critic of trade unionism.

But these contrasts are too stark. They have led to a neglect of the historical importance of Parnell's speeches after the split. It is perfectly true that Parnell made some points in this period because he *could afford to* or for the merest expediency, but at the same time they often represent his genuine convictions. With nationalist unity now a thing of the past, he was able to give vent to suppressed beliefs.

Not too much should be made of Parnell's 'republicanism' in this period. These is something gauche and unconvincing about his few remarks that fall into this category. The fact is that right up to his death he refused to admit that constitutionalism had failed. Not too much also should be made of Parnell's sudden interest in the labour question. His supporters among the Cork workingmen were dismayed in 1891 to find that he knew absolutely nothing about their local problems and aspirations (Murphy, 1979, p. 34). It seems appalling to find Parnell telling Davitt, who had questioned him about the implications of O'Shea's suit, that 'trades-unionism [was] . . . a landlordism of labour' and then to find him a few months later claiming that the future lay with the working classes. But in fact the 'landlordism of labour' remark should not be taken too literally. As Davitt himself noted (1904, pp. 636–7), 'The extraordinary opinions he gave utterance to were possibly the momentary expression of irritation at being asked a question about the divorce case, and not the reflex of his actual views on labour questions and organisations.' Nevertheless, it was for largely opportunist reasons that he sought the support of artisans and labourers, particularly in Dublin, in 1891. Republican sentiments were strong enough within this grouping, and they were among his most loyal supporters. But it is essential to note that he never advocated, even in this period, that the working class should embrace the doctrine of class struggle. Speaking in Belfast in May 1891, he noted that the manufacturing centres had been more free from industrial strife in Ulster than in any part of Great Britain:

> I do not know what the reason is. . . . I trust that labour troubles may never come amongst you, but if they do that they may be settled by mutual con- ciliation on both sides; and to the working classes I say that when mutual conciliation fails the aid of Parliament might be invoked to prevent the rude arbitrament of a strike *(cheers)*.[6]

This is the authentic voice of Parnell. Political circum- stances in 1891 apparently dictated a certain opening to the left, particularly an appeal to the labour con- stituency. Nevertheless, his words are perfectly con- sistent with his deep-rooted passion for social har- mony in the 'new Ireland'.

On the other hand, it is fair to say that Parnell did break with what might be called Catholic nationalism — as opposed to a broader non-sectarian conception which has always coexisted uneasily with it. His utter- ances on the place of Protestants within Irish politics were of piercing accuracy. In Belfast in May 1891 he went right to the heart of the matter. Parnell's speech on this occasion was surely one of the most remark- able in his career. St John Ervine justly described it as 'impressive'. The truth is that it is inconceivable that any of his major lieutenants of the 1880s could have produced so substantive an analysis of the obstacles to Irish unity.

There is no question of characterising the speech as a bitter frenetic outburst. We have a description of

Parnell's bearing on this occasion which rules out this interpretation. It come from a relatively neutral Ulster Presbyterian source:

> His style on beginning to speak, was calm, slow, telling. When he had warmed with his subject, he became more animated, and at times even warm; but on the whole his tone was reserved, cool and forcible, not a point failing to be pressed home. . . . He discussed with active calmness, moving about freely on the platform, usually in his favourite attitude, with arms folded. . . . Treating it merely as an oratorical effect, we may characterise it as being important, clear, forcible, statesmanlike.[7]

Parnell broke completely with a carping attitude towards the North's greater relative prosperity. Belfast Unionist observers were inclined to dismiss Parnell's new attitude as 'ritualistic', but the change of emphasis and tone as compared with, say, his remarks on the same subject in 1886 is remarkable.

> Now, everybody who comes to this great city and to the North of Ireland is struck by the difference that it presents to other parts of this country. . . . If I were asked to point out any portion of the world where the population are suitably distributed upon the land, I should point to the province of Ulster *(cheers)*. . . .
> Going through your great province one comes, having noted these things, upon thriving manufacturing communities — Lurgan, Portadown, and many other hives of industry — until we reach the climax of all this in this city of Belfast *(applause)*. . . . I admire the manufacturing success of Ulster — *(cheers)* — and I wish it long life and prosperity.[8]

But the nub of the speech concerned the relationship between Catholics and Protestants in a period of the political expansion of Irish nationalism. Here Parnell for the first time in his career made points which — it was to prove — were unacceptable to many of his Catholic fellow-nationalists. There is no doubt that at this juncture Parnell ceased to be the 'tame' Protestant leader of the Home Rule movement. His tone was firm yet restrained; in particular, he resisted the temptation to give the divorce crisis itself too much meaning as an index of Catholic—Protestant relationships. (And yet, when all is said and done, the crisis both revealed and increased the power of the Irish Catholic Church.) It deserved, but did not receive, serious discussion among those who took Irish unity seriously as a political objective.

I have to say this, that it is the duty of the majority to leave no stone unturned, no means unused, to conciliate the reasonable or unreasonable prejudices of the minority* *(cheers)*. I think the majority have always been inclined to go a long way in this direction; but it has been undoubtedly true that every Irish patriot has always recognised . . . from the time of Wolf[e] Tone until now that until the religious prejudices of the minority, whether reasonable or unreasonable, are conciliated . . . Ireland can never enjoy perfect freedom, Ireland can never be united; and until Ireland is practically united, so long as there is a large majority, perhaps a bare majority — in Belfast a considerable majority, in the other provinces of Ireland a majority bearing like proportion — so long as there is this important minority† who consider, rightly

*The misprint 'majority' which occurs at this point in the newspaper report of the speech has here been corrected.

†This slide from the term 'majority' to 'minority' is caused by the fact that Parnell moves from thinking of Irish Protestants in a northeast Ulster context, in which they are a majority, to an all-Ireland context, in which they are a minority.

or wrongly — I believe and feel sure wrongly — that the concession of legitimate freedom to Ireland means harm and damage to them, either to their spiritual or their temporal interests, the work of building up an independent Ireland will have upon it a fatal clog and a fatal drag *(cheers)*. I do not know, my friends, whether there are any elements in the present struggle which are likely to estrange the minority more than they have been. I trust that there are not. I trust that all Irishmen who take part in this struggle on one side or the other will see the importance of the proposition which I put before you to-night, and try to avoid doing anything to attach to this fight more than is possible, or more than is legitimate, of a sectarian or a religious aspect.[9]

Sadly, the reaction to this speech in the bulk of the nationalist press was dismissive. Parnell's 'tender consideration for the Protestant minority'[10] was noted, but without sympathy. Parnell was merely pandering to the anti-Catholic prejudices of an audience largely composed (it was dishonestly said) of Orange lodges in the 'Black North'.[11] The doctrine that there could be no legitimate freedom for Ireland until the minority was conciliated fell on unreceptive ears.[12]

The reaction of the Unionist press in Ulster is also worth recording. The agrarian radical *Derry Standard*, whose motto 'Live and Let Live' had expressed a certain ecumenism before the rise of nationalism, was particularly revealing:

Parnell said, 'I am confident, as a Protestant, and I have always been confident, there is no fear to Protestant interests from Catholic freedom.' He was the most powerful of modern Irish leaders, and yet he failed ignominiously when pitted against the priests. He is the only man in the party possessing statesmanlike qualities, and if he applied his mind seriously to the lessons from North Sligo and North Kilkenny he could not fail to learn that Protestant liberty is safer under the care of the Imperial Parliament than under an assembly elected by the priests.[13]

This is not to say that the Northern Unionists became *sotto voce* Parnellites. The reality of uneven economic development ruled that out. As the *Northern Whig* put it,

> That what is called Home Rule for Ireland, but what would not be Home Rule for Belfast and the loyal Ulster counties, would make the South and West of Ireland even comparatively as prosperous as Belfast and the districts of which it is the centre Mr Parnell assumed in his speech: but it cannot be taken for granted. Very much indeed the contrary.[14]

But they did have a new and decisive ground for characterising the nationalist movement not as a legitimate social and political movement but as the uprising of 'disloyal', priest-ridden Catholics. 'Disloyal' not just to the Empire now but to their leader. This was in a sense bitterly unfair. Many nationalists who opposed Parnell did so purely on the basis of political opposition to Parnell's disruption of the alliance with Gladstone. Nor was the influence of the Protestant clergy exactly weak in north-east Ulster. But the construction of popular ideologies has little to do with fairness. Parnell's fall was confirmation of a vision of the South which a complex of political, social and economic forces had helped to create.

It is clear that the decisive material basis — in this instance the *sine qua non* — of Ulster Unionism as a mass ideology was the uneven development of Irish

capitalism. For the loyalist bloc in Belfast it seemed
[132] incredibly obvious and 'natural' to assume that the
South's backwardness was a product not of deep-
rooted structural economic causes but of biological
inferiority, fecklessness and the influence of a grasping, oppressive church. Nature had made the Souther-
ner lazy, incapable, criminal and barbarous. It was
true that a few geniuses were produced, but they
were like solitary palms in an arid and sterile desert.
In vain did Parnell and other nationalists vigorously
contest this world-view. Ironically, the destruction
of Parnell himself appeared as positive proof of the
Northern conception. It appeared also to provide
positive proof of clerical domination in Irish politics.

The divorce crisis and its aftermath had no connection with the inevitability of partition. Ulster
Unionists had made their opposition to Home Rule
all too brutally clear some five years earlier. But it did
seem to offer evidence that the Unionist case was
justified after all. More important was the Irish
nationalist response. Even given the distaste for the
violence of Belfast Orangemen in 1886, and for
Parnell himself in 1891, that existed on the nationalist
side, the response to his Belfast speech was ill-con-
sidered and symptomatically sterile.

6

The Belfast speech was perhaps Parnell's last major
intervention in Irish politics. From early 1891 the
anti-Parnellites gloried in his physical deterioration
and hinted broadly that suicide was Parnell's next
logical move.

It was an idea that occurred to Parnell also. One
stormy evening after the divorce he and Katharine
went for a walk along Brighton pier. Parnell suddenly lifted Katharine in his arms and said: 'Oh, my

wife, my wife, I believe I'll jump with you and we shall be free forever.' Katharine responded: 'As you [133] will, my love, but the children?' This had the desired effect, for Parnell silently turned away and carried her back along the pier.

But there are other ways to die. From early 1891 everyone noticed the deterioration in Parnell's condition. An 'eyewitness' at Athlone in February, for example, wrote:

> Judging from the attenuated form, distracted looks, and unkempt appearance of the remnants left on a bald head, the fallen chieftain's days this side of the Styx are numbered. His strange appearance elicited the following expression from an old Leinster man whom he recognised and shook hands with — 'Egad, Charley, you is a done cat any minute.'[15]

All the while he was subject to the attentions of Irish crowds — often in their most spiteful mood. A couple of incidents that occurred during his trip to Mayo a month before he died may be cited as typical examples. At Castlebar he found himself surrounded by a hostile crowd:

> There was any amount of booing, hissings, calls for Kitty, Foxeen, Grouse, etc., mingled with such remarks as 'Charley I hardly knew you,' 'How is Kitty?' etc. An aged woman tried to make her way through the crowd, exclaiming 'Let me see him.' When her curiosity was satisfied she said 'You are there, you ould blackguard,' and walked away in disgust.[16]

At Westport things were hardly any better. The Parnellites commissioned an old fiddler to strike up 'God Save Ireland', but he soon broke into 'The Girl I Left Behind Me'. 'The Chief turned up the white of his eye and said "Throw that fellow off."' The

Connaught Telegraph of 12 September 1891 con-
[134] cluded by describing him as a 'relic ... all but a dead
man whom the fate of Castlereagh is awaiting'.

After a severe soaking which he received on 27
September while speaking at a meeting at Creggs, a
remote village on the borders of Galway and Roscommon, he returned home to Katharine at Brighton.
He was clearly on his last legs. He died shortly before
midnight on 6 October. Twenty-three years later his
wife could still vividly recall the exact moment of his
passing:

> Late in the evening he suddenly opened his eyes
> and said: 'Kiss me, sweet Wifie, and I will try to
> sleep a little.' I lay down by his side, and kissed
> the burning lips he pressed to mine for the last
> time. The fire of them, fierce beyond any that I
> had ever felt, even in his most loving moods,
> startled me, and as I slipped my hand from under
> his head he gave a little sigh and became uncon-
> scious. The doctor came at once, but no remedies
> prevailed against this sudden failure of the heart's
> action, and my husband died without regaining
> consciousness, before his last kiss was cold on my
> lips.

She added: 'He did not make any "dying speech" or
refer in any way to his "colleagues and the Irish
people" as was at the time erroneously reported.'

The obituaries were predictable. Most of the
English writers concentrated on the political effects
of Parnell's death. It was widely and incorrectly
assumed that now that Parnell was gone, the reuni-
fication of the Irish Parliamentary Party would be
rapidly achieved. In Ireland, however — although
everyone made some obeisance to the chastening
power of death — the tone of the recent conflict

was still present. The Parnellite Augustus Moore (1891) caught his side's sense of betrayal:

> There is but one of two fates for an Irish patriot. Unlike most Irish patriots, Mr Parnell did not sell his country and his colleagues, and the result was that his colleagues sold him. . . . Mr Parnell was not a man of much invention, eloquence or resource, but he was a gentleman; he was honest, and he was earnest, which is more than can be said of the men who deserted him for Barabbas. . . . You can't help admiring such dogged pluck as he showed in fighting, or the loyalty which he proved in marrying Mrs O'Shea.

The author and journalist Standish James O'Grady (1899) extracted the most irony from the situation:

> And surely this is a strange fact in the tragic career of the man that it was precisely the class for whom he had done most that betrayed him. 'Will you fling me to the wolves?' he cried, fighting his last battle, and the Irish farmers answered, 'We will. To the wolves with you.' The working men of the towns stood by him, and the labourers of the country, both classes which he injured, while the gentry, to whom he had been an enemy, observed a neutrality which was certainly on the whole benevolent.

However, it was left to one of the anti-Parnellites, Jasper Tully, to provide the most dispassionate, generous and perceptive judgment:

> He was our own, and his faults were those we ourselves had made for him. If he was ambitious and self-willed, it was because the Irish race spoiled and petted him as never they petted a leader before.[17]

7
Conclusion

For some reason not easy to comprehend we hate perfection; we find it insipid, and all Parnell's weaknesses and foibles throw into grander relief his all but sovereign power.

STANDISH JAMES O'GRADY, 'Charles Stewart Parnell',
Kilkenny Moderator, 1 Feb. 1899

1

Many contemporaries — even sober ones —saw Parnell as a neo-republican deeply embroiled in separatist designs and as a social radical totally lacking in respect for the rights of property. We can see that, whatever his contingent alliances, Parnell's personal beliefs were rather different. He was, in fact, a conservative, constitutional nationalist with a radical tinge.

The basis of this radicalism was Parnell's concern with the fate of the Irish peasantry and, associated with this, his hopes for Irish industrial development. He was himself a generous paternalistic landlord. 'I wish I could do something for the Irish peasantry — they are worth helping,' he said to Katharine. 'I have always wished it, but there is so much between, and they suffer in silence.' (O'Shea 1914, II, p. 269).

His conservatism was perceived by at least some of his acquaintances. Augustus Moore (1891) noticed it: 'My Father [George Henry Moore] always was a strong Tory and a supporter of Mr Disraeli on all except Irish politics. Parnell's policy was my Father's policy.' Labouchere (1891) agreed: 'Home Rule apart, he was himself a Tory.'

His main disagreement with the British Conservatives was their refusal to follow a truly conservative policy on Ireland. As he pointed out to Barry O'Brien, the British Tories were quite prepared to let the Irish landlords sink without trace. Parnell hoped this would not happen. For Parnell, the genuinely conservative settlement of the Irish question required a Dublin parliament.

But what was this Parnellite nationalism? 'No man has the right to set a boundary to the onward march of a nation,' is, of course, one of his most famous declarations. But how did he conceive the nation? Michael Tierney was to claim that 'When Parnell refused to put bounds to the march of the nation, he simply meant that he did not really know what, in the political sense, the nation wanted.'[1] Eamon de Valera, the dominating figure of independent Irish politics offered a more confident and triumphalist interpretation of Parnellism: 'All that Parnell wanted and more than he felt it expedient to demand in his day have been secured for this part of Ireland,' he told a Parnell commemoration gathering at Creggs, Co. Roscommon, on 29 December 1946. '...Our "eyes have seen the glory" which Parnell ... longed for and strove for but did not see.'[2] But Parnell's 'glory' was certainly not that mystic Celtic culture nor that Catholic peasant Ireland which was so dear to de Valera's heart. According to Tim Healy (1928, II, p. 401), his distaste for Gaelic scholarship was so pronounced as to be almost rude; and while he certainly felt a sense of duty towards the unfortunate sections of the Irish peasantry, there is no sign that he regarded them on religious or any other grounds as particularly fine exemplars of humanity.

Parnell's nationalism resided basically in a faith in the superior capacity of Ireland's local ruling class — as compared with the incompetence of the English administration — to control the inhabitants. But this is merely the site of the problem: for who was to be the ruling class? The nascent domestic Irish Catholic [138] bourgeoisie or its literary or legal representatives was decidedly not Parnell's *first* choice. He did not wish it to be the exclusively dominating force within the new dispensation of power. As he put it to Kettle (1958, p. 63), 'I have to work with the tools that come to my hand. I have no choice. The men I would like to have won't come, so I have to use the men who will.'

This is the paradox of Parnellism. He desperately sought a reconciliation between the Catholic democracy and the Southern Irish Protestant ascendancy, but he failed to achieve it. In fact the time was not ripe for such a compromise. As one shrewd pro-landlord commentator acknowledged in 1881, the chance had really been missed at an earlier stage, the period of Butt's dominance. In the words of this writer,

> Elated with an absolute power which had lasted for centuries; blind to the fact that their political influence was going, if not gone; forgetful of the fact they were only a minority; the friends of England in a country where England was hated, the Irish aristocracy laughed at Mr Butt and refused to leave a position which political power alone could have retained for them.[3]

Parnell was no less desirous of winning over the landlords than Butt was; however, in his time elemental forces were at work which made a compromise doubly difficult to achieve. Indeed, as the agrarian class conflict intensified, the terms Parnell was able to offer deteriorated all the while. As he reminded the Irish landlords in 1891, 'the terms which they scoffed at or ridiculed in 1879, they would be only too glad to obtain today'.[4] But in 1886, and again in 1890 and 1891, Parnell did his best to get his fellow-landlords 'off the hook'.

Parnell was decidedly less consistent in his attitude [139] towards the large Protestant community in the North. In the early part of his career he had not been much interested in Ulster. He tended to treat the Ulster Protestants as though they constituted a solid but insignificant bloc of bigotry and reaction. But a sophisticated patrician's cold disdain is no substitute for analysis and action.

Parnell had been slow to see the importance of attempting to neutralise the Presbyterian 'Whig' agrarian radical element in Ulster. In February 1878 he had been among those thirty-five Home Rule MPs censured by *The Nation* for failing to vote for Ulster land reform proposals at Westminster. Later, during the land war in 1881, one of his close lieutenants, J. J. O'Kelly, urged that nothing should be done to alienate this potentially sympathetic group of Northern radicals. Parnell, however, against the advice of both O'Kelly and Kettle, put up a Nationalist candidate in Tyrone, an action which, in O'Kelly's words, 'alarmed and angered the whole Presbyterian body, and split Ulster once more into distinctly hostile camps of Catholic and Protestant'. (O'Brien and Ryan, 1948–53, II, pp. 142–3).

In March 1885 he had said of the nascent Ulster Unionist movement:

I call them the English party in Ireland because I think that more correctly designates them than the title of 'loyal minority' which they have assumed. . . . No doubt there had been and still were brave men among them (hear, hear); but on the whole they had shown themselves to be a selfish and inconsiderate race mindful only of their own interests (*cheers*).[5]

In November of that year he had gone on to say:

> I absolutely deny that Ulster is the most industrious province. I have never seen anything in any country to equal the indefatigable toil of the Connaught peasant, who has reclaimed the mountains and the marshes . . . and who migrates every year to England and Scotland to find in the cornfields and gardens of those countries that employment which is denied to him at home.[6]

Parnell was merely reflecting widespread nationalist sentiment here. The *Connaught Telegraph* put it more bitterly:

> We have been told in the canny Scotch *patois* of the oily souper that the obvious cause of peace and plenty in one region and crime and misery in the other, originated and centred on the fact that Protestantism dignified the former and Catholicism impoverished the latter.[7]

What these remarks indicate is a culture clash of enormous proportions. Parnell in the years 1885–86 simply lacked the intelligence, sympathy or vision – especially when confronted with Orange anti-Catholic violence in Belfast – to produce a political line that would allay the fears of Northern Protestants.

By the late 1880s Parnell seems at last to have realised that his conciliatory approach towards the landlords ought to be extended to Ulster Protestants as well. It is necessary to stress this, because the current phase of the Irish troubles has tended to create a more critical attitude towards Parnell. The sharpest censures of the Irish leader have been those made on account of his record on the issues which seem most relevant to the present conflict between Protestants and Catholics in Northern Ireland.

In 1957 Conor Cruise O'Brien felt able to claim in his *Parnell and his Party, 1880–1890* (p. 157):

> It would be unsafe to say that an English majority led by Gladstone and an Irish majority led by Parnell could not — especially in the favourable climate of opinion created by the exposure in 1889 of the forgeries published by *The Times* — have achieved a settlement which preserved Irish unity.

But in 1978 the same writer has commented on Parnell in a very different tone: 'He could not . . . ever have "won Home Rule", because Home Rule was simply not winnable. Parnell, though a Protestant, was speaking for the Catholics of Ireland, not — as he and his followers appeared to take for granted — for an Irish nation that included the Ulster Protestants.'[8] In his recent biography F. S. L. Lyons (1977, p. 623) has observed sharply that Parnell

> seems never to have asked himself what he meant by the 'Irish nation' or the 'Irish race' which he claimed to lead, and the idea that Ireland might possibly contain two nations, not one, apparently never entered his head.

Lyons says of Parnell's position on Ulster Unionism that he 'never came remotely within reach of developing a constructive approach to the potentially lethal threat it represented'.

In partial defence of Parnell, Nicholas Mansergh (1978, pp. 13–14) has argued in this context that there was a real possibility that a 'two nations' line on the part of constitutional leaders might simply have hastened a revolutionary takeover of nationalist politics. He has further commented on Parnell's 'one nation' position: 'From such assumptions of unity may have derived many of the insensitivities which confirmed partition, but how far did they

cause it?' Mansergh here is signalling an important
[142] fact: there were strong forces making for a partition
settlement regardless of the line adopted by the
nationalist leaders. This is a weighty argument, but
it is not the one pursued here. For it is still reasonable
to insist, as Lyons does, that as the dimensions of
Ulster Unionist resistance to Home Rule were clear
enough before Parnell's death, he ought to have
offered some serious reflections on the subject.

This study has argued that Parnell, as a Protestant
himself, was intensely concerned about the place of
Irish Protestants in the national life. *This is the
neglected clue to Parnell's political career.* Most
of this concern was directed towards Parnell's 'own
people', the Southern Irish Protestants. His interest
in the Northern Protestants was much less marked;
he found it difficult to identify with them, and for
most of his career his views on their role and problems
were uninformed and ill conceptualised. Yet, as has
been shown, after this slow and unpromising start
he offered what ought to have been seminal suggestions concerning attitudes to the Ulster Unionist
movement. By 1891 he was openly stating that

> It has been undoubtedly true that every Irish
> patriot has always recognised . . . from the time
> of Wolf[e] Tone until now that until the religious
> prejudices of the minority, whether reasonable
> or unreasonable, are conciliated . . . Ireland can
> never enjoy perfect freedom, Ireland can never be
> united.[9]

This suggestive statement might stand rather better
on Parnell's statue in Dublin than the windy blast of
'patriotic' rhetoric which at present adorns it.

But if this is the correct interpretation of Parnell's
politics on the Ulster question, what are the implications? Parnell's most explicit statements on this point

occur *after* the divorce crisis. It can be argued that only then could Parnell afford to say such things. While he was still the leader of a united nationalist contingent such arguments would have been highly divisive. In other words, Parnell's attack on his party's traditional views on Ulster in 1891 may be regarded as a proof that he was virtually the captive of Catholic nationalism during the entire period when he was supposed to be its unrivalled autocratic leader.

3

The clue to Parnell's rise was the land war. It was this struggle which turned him from a coming young man into the 'uncrowned King of Ireland'. The sudden and dramatic effects of the Land League are clear: at the beginning of 1880 Irish landlordism was intact; by the spring of 1881 it was clear to friend and foe that it was doomed.

Once the masses got involved in politics — as they did in the period 1879—82 — all the 'leaders' were swept along. They all had their hopes for the outcome of the agitation, but nobody was in a position to impose a solution — Fenian, constitutional, clerical or otherwise. The price of non-involvement was total irrelevance. *It was the action of the people which imposed a unity of sorts on the leadership.* By 1882 Parnell was the symbol of that unity, but it was forged not of genuine consensus but out of the exhaustion of the competing forces. Specifically Fenian hopes for a revolutionary outcome to the agrarian conflict had been disappointed, and some turned in bitterness to terrorism. On the other hand, 'moderates' now had to work with men they had previously shunned. 'The Chief' was uncomfortably aware that while he was the focus of national sentiment, he was by no means in control of it. By 1882 the very turbulence of the agitation had convinced him of the need to strengthen the more conservative forces in Irish political life. He began the business of providing the machinery — which was strongly influenced by the Catholic clergy — for a constitutional agitation aimed at Home Rule rather than an agrarian revolution. It is only fair to say that Parnell's room for manoeuvre was weakened by those republican militants who, rather than struggle *politically* for those non-sectarian national ideals to which they were in principle dedicated, involved themselves in acts of terrorism. The shocking crime in Phoenix Park in 1882 and the subsequent dynamite outrages in 1883 and 1884 were significant incentives to quieter politics. Parnell was thus pushed towards the 'right centre' of Irish politics.

There were powerful political reasons making for this choice and, once made, for sticking to it. The 1880s saw a major change in the Anglo-Irish balance of power. This is all the more impressive when compared with the futile squabbling and disunity of the nationalist forces in the 1870s. Yet this cannot disguise the fact that the much-vaunted unity of the Parnellite bloc was bought at a price — and part of that price was the leader's self-censorship. Barry O'Brien (1898, I, pp. 103–4) has commented: 'No quarrels was certainly a favourite thought, if not a favourite expression of Parnell. To have any single force which made for Irish nationality in conflict with any force which could be made in the same direction was utterly abhorrent.' But there could be no real unity between those who saw the ethos of the new Ireland as being specifically Catholic and peasant and a Protestant squire who wanted to save the remnants of his class from the ravages of history. The price for this false unanimity was paid by Parnell personally. His project of integrating

Irish Protestants with the new order of things in Ireland was kept alive only in fits and starts. The ideal of an autonomous, peaceful, pluralistic country eluded him totally; more importantly, it has also eluded later generations.

Parnell's great flaw, of course, remains. The O'Shea liaison was reckless in the extreme. But it can now be seen in a different light. Too often in the years after 1882, when he might have fought actively for his ideal, Parnell lingered in Eltham. He saw the problem — that of sectarian division in the Irish people. He early grasped the nature of this problem in the South; belatedly he appreciated its full significance in the North. But he intervened only fitfully before his last great fight. He surrendered, not the leadership, but much of the initiative, to other, inferior hands. There are excuses: an overwhelming disgust with terrorism is one, and illness is another. But in the end it must be said that by his own lights he was inadequate.

References

Chapter 1: 'The Accident of Birth' (pp. 4—15)
1. Owen Roe, 'Thomas Parnell' (Hours with Irish Poets, No. X), *Nation*, 4 Nov. 1876.
2. *Freeman's Journal*, 8 Oct. 1891.
3. *Nation*, 31 Jan. 1885.

Chapter 2: 'On the Verge of Treason-Felony' (pp. 16—30)
1. *Roscommon Herald*, 30 Apr. 1887.
2. *Meath Herald*, 24 Apr. 1875.
3. *Ibid.*
4. *Kilkenny Moderator*, 7 Apr. 1875.
5. *Irishman*, 24 Apr. 1875.   6. *Ibid.*, 20 Nov. 1875.
7. *Ibid.*, 8 Jan. 1876.   8. *Ibid.*, 15 Jan. 1876.
9. *Ibid.*, 21 Jun. 1877.   10. *Ibid.*, 25 Aug. 1877.
11. J. Kilmartin, 'The Political Situation', *Tuam News*, 2 Jan. 1891.
12. *Limerick Reporter*, 2, 30 Jan., 5 Jun., 23 Jul., 21 Aug. 1877.
13. *Connaught Telegraph*, 15 Dec. 1877.
14. *Weekly Freeman*, 25 Apr. 1891.
15. Kilmartin in *Tuam News*, 2 Jan. 1891.
16. *Nation*, 9 Nov. 1878.
17. Quoted in Bew, *Land and the National Question*, 52.
18. Both contributions to the debate appear in *Nation*, 9 Feb. 1878.
19. *Ibid.*, 23 Nov. 1878.   20. *Ibid.*, 9 Feb. 1878.

Chapter 3: 'A Spontaneous Uprising': The Land League (pp. 30—65)
1. Butt to Cairnes, 14 Nov. 1872 (NLI, Cairnes Papers, MS. 8944).
2. *Freeman's Journal*, 1 Dec. 1879.
3. *Connaught Telegraph*, 20, 27 Jan. 1877.
4. *Freeman's Journal*, 20 Apr. 1890.
5. Quoted in Bew, 78.
6. 'Mr Parnell's Connection with Cork', *Cork Daily Herald*, 6 Oct. 1891.
7. *Roscommon Herald*, 17 Jan. 1891.
8. Quoted in Bew, 108.   9. *Nation*, 2 Jan, 1886.
10. *Daily Mail*, 18 May 1914.

11. *Freeman's Journal*, 27 Sep. 1880.

12. *Kilkenny Moderator*, 13 Aug. 1898.

13. *Roscommon Messenger*, 3 Oct. 1891.

14. *Dundalk Democrat*, 30 Jun. 1883; see also *People's Advocate* (Monaghan), 7 Jul. 1883.

15. K. O'Shea to Gladstone, 19 Jul. 1883 (BM, Gladstone Papers, Add. MS. 44420).

16. *Tuam News*, 25 Apr., 16, 30 May 1884.

17. *Nation*, 30 May 1885.

Chapter 4: 'He Knew What He Wanted': Home Rule in 1886 (pp. 65—92)

1. *Nation*, 31 Jan. 1885.   2. *Ibid.*, 17 Oct. 1885.

3. Parnell to K. O'Shea, 6 Jan. 1886 (BM, Gladstone Papers, Add. MS. 44629); see also Parnell to E. D. Gray, 3 Jan. 1885 (NLI, MS. 15735).

4. Quoted in Dunne, 'The Political Ideology of Home Rule', 209—10; see also Vincent, *Gladstone and Ireland*.

5. Gladstone to Harcourt, 12 Feb. 1886 (Bodl., Harcourt Papers, deposit box 10).

6. See *Northern Whig*, 16—17 Apr. 1886, for a useful discussion of these points.

7. *Ibid.*

8. *Freeman's Journal*, 22 Apr. 1880.

9. *Nation*, 28 Aug. 1886.

Chapter 5: 'The Bitterness of Party Conflict': 'Parnellism and Crime' (pp. 92—112)

1. *Munster Express*, 26 Nov. 1887.

2. *Roscommon Herald*, 13 Dec. 1890.

3. Quoted *ibid.*, 4 Aug. 1889.

Chapter 6: 'Sticking to His corner' (pp. 112—35)

1. *Freeman's Journal*, 11 Dec. 1890.   2. *Ibid*.

3. *Roscommon Herald*, 21 Feb. 1891.

4. *Connaught Telegraph*, 9 May 1891.

5. *Roscommon Herald*, 20 Dec. 1890.

6. *Witness*, 29 May 1891.   7. *Ibid*.

8. *Northern Whig*, 23 May 1891.   9. *Ibid*.

10. *Cork Examiner*, 25 May 1891.

11. *Cork Weekly Herald*, 30 May 1891.

12. *Munster News*, 23 May 1891.

13. *Derry Standard*, 25 May 1891.

14. *Northern Whig*, 23 May 1891.

15. *Connaught Telegraph*, 24 Feb. 1891.

16. *Ibid.*, 12 Sep. 1891.

17. *Roscommon Herald*, 10 Oct. 1891.

[148] Chapter 7: Conclusion (pp. 136—45)
 1. M. Tierney, 'A Prophet of Mystic Nationalism — AE', *Studies* XXVI, Pt 4 (1937), 573.
 2. *Irish Times*, 30 Dec. 1946.
 3. *Kilkenny Moderator*, 26 Oct. 1891. (The author is almost certainly Standish James O'Grady.)
 4. *Roscommon Messenger*, 25 Jul. 1891.
 5. *Nation*, 14 Mar. 1885.   6. *Ibid.*, 14 Nov. 1885.
 7. *Connaught Telegraph*, 5 Mar. 1879.
 8. C. C. O'Brien, Review of Foster, *Charles Stewart Parnell: The Man and his Family*, and Lyons, *Charles Stewart Parnell* in *Irish Historical Studies* XX, No. 80 (Sep. 1977), 518.
 9. *Northern Whig*, 23 May 1891; see also pp. 129—30 above.

Bibliography

Bew, Paul, *Land and the National Question in Ireland, 1858—82,* Dublin 1978

Blake, J. A., 'C. S. Parnell', *Nation,* 6 Jun. 1885

Davitt, Michael, *The Fall of Feudalism in Ireland, or The Story of the Land League Revolution,* London and New York 1904

Dunne, T. J., 'The Political Ideology of Home Rule' (MA thesis, University College, Dublin, 1972)

Ervine, St John, *Parnell,* London 1925

Feingold, W. L., 'Irish Boards of Poor Law Guardians: A Revolution in Local Government' (PhD thesis, University of Chicago, 1974)

Hammond, J. L., *Gladstone and the Irish Nation,* London 1938

Harrison, Henry, *Parnell Vindicated: The Lifting of the Veil,* London 1931

Healy, T. M., *Letters and Leaders of My Day,* 2 vols, London 1928

Jones, D. S., 'Agrarian Capitalism and Rural Social Development in Ireland' (PhD thesis, Queen's University, Belfast, 1978)

Kettle, A. J., *The Material for Victory,* ed. L. J. Kettle, Dublin 1958 (from a manuscript prepared by A. J. Kettle a few years before his death in 1916)

Labouchere, Henry, Parnell obituary, *Truth,* 15 Oct. 1891

Larkin, Emmet, *The Roman Catholic Church and the Fall of Parnell*, Liverpool 1979

Loughlin, J. P., 'Anglo-Saxonism and Home Rule', *Retrospect* (1979)

Lyons, F. S. L., *Charles Stewart Parnell*, London 1977

Lyons, F. S. L., *Culture and Anarchy in Ireland, 1890—1939*, Oxford 1979

McCarthy, M. J. F., *Priests and People in Ireland*, Dublin 1902

Mansergh, P. N. S., *The Prelude to Partition: Concepts and Aims in Ireland and India*, Cambridge 1978

Moore, Augustus, 'Parnell and George Henry Moore', *Tuam Herald*, 17 Oct. 1891

Morley, John, *Recollections*, 2 vols, London 1905

Murphy, Maura, 'Fenianism, Parnellism and the Cork Trades, 1860—1900', *Saothar* V (May 1979)

O'Brien, Conor Cruise, *Parnell and his Party, 1880—1890*, Oxford 1957

O'Brien, R. Barry, *The Life of Charles Stewart Parnell, 1846—1891*, 2 vols, London 1898

O'Brien, William, *The Irish Revolution*, Dublin 1923·

O'Brien, William, *The Parnell of Real Life*, London 1926

O'Brien, William, and Ryan, Desmond, ed., *Devoy's Post-Bag, 1871—1928*, 2 vols, Dublin 1948—53

O'Connor, T. P., *The Parnell Movement*, London 1887

O'Connor, T. P., *Charles Stewart Parnell: A Memory*, London 1891

O'Connor, T. P., *Memoirs of an Old Parliamentarian*, 2 vols, London 1929

O'Donnell, F. H., *A History of the Irish Parliamentary Party*, 2 vols, London 1910

O'Grady, Standish James, 'Charles Stewart Parnell', *Kilkenny Moderator*, 1 Feb. 1899

O'Malley, William, Parnell obituary, *Tuam Herald*, 17 Oct. 1891.

O'Shea, Katharine [Mrs C. S. Parnell], *Charles Stewart Parnell: His Love Story and Political Life*, 2 vols, London 1914

Parnell, J. H., *Charles Stewart Parnell: A Memoir*, London 1916

Powell, Enoch, 'Kilmainham — the Treaty that Never Was', *Historical Journal* XXI, No. 4 (1978)

Raymond, Raymond J., ed., 'Some Recently Discovered Parnell Letters', *Éire — Ireland* (forthcoming, 1980)

Robbins, Sir Alfred, *Parnell: The Last Five Years*, London 1926

Shaw, J. J., *Mr Gladstone's Two Irish Policies: 1868 and 1886*, Belfast 1888

[150] Sherlock, T., *Charles Stewart Parnell*, Dublin 1887 (originally published Boston 1881)

Tuohy, J. M., 'The Death of Mr Parnell', *Freeman's Journal*, 8 Oct. 1891

Vincent, J. R., *Gladstone and Ireland*, London 1979

Zubof, Count Roman, 'A Glance at Parnell', reprinted in *Tuam Herald*, 7 Mar. 1891

Index